M000014936

SECOND PASSPORT

Your Guide to a Secure Alternative Home for You and Your Family, Just in Case...

Brandon Miller

Copyright © Brandon Miller, 2019

All rights reserved. No part of this book may be reproduced in any form without permission in writing from the author. Reviewers may quote brief passages in reviews.

Published 2019

DISCLAIMER

No part of this publication may be reproduced or transmitted in any form or by any means, mechanical or electronic, including photocopying or recording, or by any information storage and retrieval system, or transmitted by email without permission in writing from the author.

Immigration to Canada and all aspects related to moving/relocating to a new country are complicated. Due to the personalized and unique nature of an individual and/or their family's situation there are several factors that need to be considered. The information contained in this book is for general information purposes and does not constitute legal advice. Neither the author; the publisher, nor any associated companies; people; or legal entities assume any responsibility whatsoever for errors, omissions, or contrary interpretations of the subject matter herein. Any perceived slight of any individual or organization is purely unintentional.

Professional advice from competent and legally entitled authorities is always advised and choosing to engage such services is at the discretion of the reader. The reader will assume any and all liability should they wish to utilize the information contained in this publication or any associated partner materials found within this book or through companion resources. Immigration law and other associated laws are complicated, change from time to time, and the information in this book is based on the author's personal experiences and opinions and should be construed as nothing more than this.

Some of the events described happened as related, others were expanded and changed. The names and other identifying characteristics of the persons included in this book have been changed. Throughout this book I have used examples from many of my clients' personal lives. However, to ensure privacy and confidentiality I have changed some of their names and some of the details of their experience. All the personal examples of my own life have not been altered.

If you would like further information about Maple Immigration Services or Second Passport Programs, please call +1-647-748-8472 (Visa) or 1-844-VISA-HERE

Brand and product names are trademarks or registered trademarks of their respective owners.

ACKNOWLEDGMENTS

Foremost, I am thankful to all of my clients who have shaped me and allowed me to grow into the person I am today while graciously welcoming me into their lives.

To my daughters, Samantha and Allison, you mean more to me than words can even express, you are the very reason that I am driven to be who I am. I want nothing more than to be a positive influence and role model that you can be proud of. To my parents, I know I was a handful, and you did the best that you could with me, especially my mother who was always positive and super supportive. Ryan, you stood by me in thick and thin, even at times to your own detriment and frustration. Your unconditional love and support have meant more to me than you'll ever know.

The Maple team, both past and present, you mean so much to me as without you, we would not have been able to grow in the manner that we have, nor would we have been able to set ourselves up to create a more positive impact in the world for our clients.

To all of the people who I have done business with in the past, you have made me who I am today. Kory; Patti; Dan; the Coach team; and all of the people who have invested the time to learn with me, your ever-positive energy and support have meant the world to me. My archangel family, I am super grateful for all of the support and guidance that you have given so as to allow me to truly expand my positive impact on the world. To Angela and her team, who took the time to let me see what was possible in getting my message out there.

To all of my colleagues and mentors in the immigration profession who have welcomed me into an industry. You have shown me what advocating is all about and have allowed me to increase my positive footprint in the world.

Specifically to John for helping to cultivate my love of corned beef sandwiches; Monica for tolerating my potty mouth; Norbert and Katina my "interns" who I now look to and continue to be impressed with; Rhonda, Elda, and Elizabeth who taught me that a collegial world can and should exist more with our government counterparts. Roxanne, I am more grateful than you'll ever know for the Saturday morning group, where you took your time to bring all of us up to the standards of true professionals. You're a friend, mentor, a hero and I think the world of you.

Lastly, to the love of my life, Ilien, I would not be the man I am today without you. I am blessed that we are on this journey together, happy to call you my partner in all aspects of life, grateful that we have endured and continue to endure our struggles to grow stronger. You have pushed me to grow so that I am able to be the best version of myself.

CONTENTS

CHAPTER 1:

WHY CANADA IS THE PLACE TO BE

So, you have decided that you are going to press forward and make Canada your home. *Awesome!* I am so proud of your decision, as Canada is always welcoming talented and forward-thinking people who believe in settling in a peaceful place and adding to the diversity that we are happy to have here! I know that you have looked around and may or may not have decided that this is for you and for your family. You are looking for safety and security. You are seeking openness and opportunity for yourself and for your family to grow in. Maybe you have been looking for something more, or maybe there is something in the back of your mind that calls you to Canada or to this book for that matter. Whatever it is – you are here, and I am thankful that you are.

I want you to keep reading so that I can guide you on how you can start your new life in Canada and make this dream actually come true. I hope that by doing this, you will be fully educated on the Canadian immigration system, and that you will know the questions that you should be asking before coming to Canada and while you're filling out the application. From this book, it is my sincere hope that you will have an understanding of what it takes to make that plan and, most importantly, how to execute and make it happen, as this is what life is all about. We all know that having a plan and making it happen is the only reason that you have been so successful at this point in life, and this process is no different. I am here to help guide you through this and give you a systematic plan that you are able to execute, so that you immigrate and settle successfully.

Prior to diving into the "how" to come to Canada portion of this book, I would really like to set the stage and give you some information about the *why*.

I know that people have a few reasons for why they want to come to Canada, but I would like to delve deeper into this and give you some of the most common reasons that I've heard from my clients over the years about why they come here. Also, it is my intention to give you some other things to think about.

BACKGROUND OF CANADA AND IMMIGRATION TO CANADA

There is a reason that Canada rates so highly on the indexes that come out around the world, and no it is not because we are bribing the writers with free Tim Hortons coffee and poutine. It is because this really is an awesome place to live. I am very blessed to know this. You will hear the same thing from people who have lived here their whole lives and never travelled (except maybe to an all-inclusive vacation bubble down in Mexico), but I have spent a good chunk of my life living and travelling overseas, so I actually have context of why this is.

Canada is a free place for you to live peacefully with your family and do whatever you wish, as long as you do not infringe on another person's right to do the same thing. That is it – that's our secret – oh, and we give out free chocolate and ice cream on Wednesdays!

We are a nation of immigrants and the diversity is embraced. You may or may not be familiar with the terms *"melting pot"* and *"mosaic."* But these are very special terms that are taught in school at a very young age that are key to understanding Canada. We are a mosaic, which means that we are made up of a bunch of different cultures and religions, and this forms the basis of what and who we are. A melting pot is when you go to a new country, you assume their identity, and you're committed to stripping your own previous history or identity. Take a minute to thank about how powerful that actually is. I know I do, and I think that it is so powerful to be acknowledged for who you are and where you came from while coming together to embrace your new home.

I also find that Canada has increasingly become more and more of a logical choice for people to come to settle in, and this is because of what is happening in the world today. At the time of writing this book, we are seeing increasing instability in the world in places that have traditionally been stable, and I have seen and will continue to see an increase of people inquiring about coming to Canada. Why? Because we are all the same, and we all want nothing more than what you want – a safe secure place to settle with your family where you can have a bright future.

I don't want to make this book about why the world is so scary, but I would like to point out that in an increasing world of confusion and uncertainty, with some radical leaders and policies that are dominating the discourse we see today, Canada still remains to be a bastion, and our leaders have held on to their moral compass, while staying true to the values that we hold dear as Canadians.

Let's shift gears for a minute and let me give you some of the more popular reasons that I have heard from people/clients over the years about why they want to come to Canada and their reasons for looking to settle here.

SECURITY

Some people are looking at their homelands or where they are living currently and seeing an increasing number of security risks to themselves and, more importantly, to their families. Whether this is lack of law and protection, or bigger threats from other foreign powers, this by far is one of the most popular reasons that I hear for wanting to come to Canada. I have even heard this from Americans, who are seeing all of the gun issues and the rising number of mass shootings as a very real concern for their safety. People are starting to be *very* concerned in this respect about safety and security for them and their family.

FINANCIAL

I hear a lot from people that they are looking for greater job prospects or they are moving for some sort of financial reason. Of course, this is more paramount for some people and also a very real concern. Depending on where you come from, you can hold on to your money better and also if you have a good accountant you will see this grow. There is a presumption here in Canada that your income will be taxed, and yes, this is true, as we need to pay for all of the great benefits that we have. But if you actually look at it, the taxes are not that bad, and there are ways to make it easier, like using a professional accountant that can help you hold on to more of your money and also use it wisely.

HEALTH

We have health care as a basic right in this country, and that, for a number of people, is reason enough to look to Canada as an option. Our health care system and values demand that people have access to care, and this is not a political issue that we are still trying to sort out. You can be rest assured that while you are living in Canada, you will have the ability to see a doctor and get medical treatments that are necessary to meet your basic health needs, and that you and your family will not need to figure out how you will pay for a life-saving treatment.

THE LOGICAL CHOICE IN THE WESTERN WORLD

We are seen as the logical choice in the western/first world, due to our openness and liberal policies that allow people to come and still keep their identities. Also, we are less rigid with second passport holders. We also are not a far stretch from people's homelands, as it is very easy to find a piece of your birthplace in any major urban center.

For some, (and I am thinking of my American clients) you will find that living in Canada is no different than living in the US – except for a few different accent intonations and a brighter colored collection of bank notes. However, you may be disappointed that the chocolate bar combinations are way more diverse in the US!

TAXATION / WEALTH PRESERVATION

Some clients who amass a great deal of wealth feel that they're in danger of it being taken away, as is the case with some countries that I have been in, where the country is breaking down and they need to hold on to foreign currency and not allow the currency to leave, or others who have had state-controlled entities come in and take over their business. Yes, these things happen (usually very quietly and in various levels of threat) I know first-hand as I have worked with clients who have been in the very uncomfortable predicament. Nonetheless, people are trying to preserve that which they have worked hard to build, and whether they are being "shaken down" by an authoritarian regime, or legally by the tax man, they can strategically look at moving to Canada as an option for them or as one of the pillars of their *Flag Theory Plan*, should they choose that life.

RESOURCES AND THE ENVIRONMENT

I have heard this argument advanced a few times and in different ways. It was very surprising for me in the beginning, but in looking at it and where the world is going these days, it is becoming more real. I recall the first time that I heard this from someone who was from China and trying to decide weather to go to Canada or Australia, and she made the choice to come to Canada because of the fresh water supply. She felt that Australia would not have this for long, and that they were heading toward becoming a desert. I have also heard about global warming and storm patterns, and how we are seeing more insulation in less coastal areas of the country, and how people are looking at this in terms of their long-term settlement. For me, I believe that this is quite a valid argument. If you look at what will happen to places where there is high population and shrinking land, where vacuums of leadership tend to not exist, then there will be issues going forward that do not paint a very pretty picture.

FREEDOM

This is more of an obvious one for someone who does not come from a free society. They dream of being free to do what they want, when they want, or they are worried and not able to be themselves because they are being watched all the time. All governments do this, and it is increasingly easier for them to do it, but it is all about the safeguards that are in places and the abuse that takes place when these tools come into play. In Canada we still have mechanisms in place to limit the encroachment of our freedoms by the government.

MORAL ARGUMENT

I have heard an argument made that people object to certain things that their government is doing. For instance, they morally object to having their tax dollars used for abortion, or they object to a conflict that their country is involved in. This is not one of the most popular reasons, but we have seen these arguments pop up from time to time. I recall growing up with someone whose father fled the United States because he was a moral objector to the Vietnam War and they settled in Canada with the family.

BENEFITS

There are numerous benefits, some of which have already been touched on in this chapter, but I also think that we should look at this very pragmatically, as there are some very real benefits to having a Canadian passport.

SAFETY IN THE WORLD WHEN TRAVELLING

There is no better comfort that I have when traveling around the world, than knowing that I have a Canadian passport. I have travelled with friends from South of the border who, when asked, would say that they were from Canada, because they felt that it was "just easier". Originally, I was quite surprised by this, but I have seen first-hand the change in the tone of the conversation when confronted with this. I also have seen people have issues with the law overseas and have witnessed the difference in treatment they receive when they are in a foreign jail or detention. I know that, in some places, a Canadian passport has saved them from very bad treatment. I personally did not travel to some areas of the world with my wife until she had her Canadian passport, on the off chance that we needed counselor services. Reason being is that I knew that the level of service she would have received from her home country, as opposed to the Canadian embassy, would be night and day and would have left her in a very tough spot.

EDUCATION

We have, arguably, a pretty good and very cost-effective subsidized education system here in Canada. I know that I have had some clients who were unhappy with what they were spending on student fees at top tier schools in their home country, and end up immigrating to Canada so that they can have access to good education for their children, and also easier routes into post-secondary education. We have free education up to grade twelve (high school or secondary school), and then our post-secondary education is highly subsidized and affordable, while at the same time supported by *very* gracious loans for people to be able to study. In Canada, we value an educated population, and this is supported.

WORKER AND TRAVELER MOBILITY

This is something that is quite overlooked, but if you start looking into the ease of working and travelling around the world with a Canadian passport, you will find that this opens up a number of opportunities. Canada has a huge number of reciprocal working arrangements that allow people to work in Canada. These arrangements also allow Canadians of any age to travel and work in several different countries, only because they have Canadian citizenship. There are a number of opportunities that are out there for people, and having a Canadian passport allows you to work in many different countries and travel freely as you will not be subjected to visa restrictions. You can take full advantage of, not only what Canada has to offer, but other opportunities in the world as well. To underscore this, I look at how people are paid in the Middle East for instance – Indian workers know this – that if they have the exact same job as an Indian national, they are paid a lower rate, should they come back to the exact same job with the exact same skill set and have a Canadian passport, their wage will be significantly higher.

HEALTH CARE AND LIFE SPAN

Presumably, if you are being taken care of and you are not being asked to sacrifice your health due to not being able to afford treatment (as we see health care as a basic human right), you should live longer. Canada tends to have a better environment, a stable and trustworthy food supply, and I believe that this all contributes to a longer life span. For many years, we have contributed to the advancing of medical knowledge (you're welcome for the discovery of insulin) and this has not stopped today. I like to speak about lifespan with people because it really hits home, as we all have a common goal to live longer, and Canada is certainly a leader in this respect. If you take someone from, say India or the Philippines, just moving to Canada can add up to fourteen years to their life span. This to me could be the *only* argument needed for moving here, as this will cost you otherwise with what should be most important to you.

RETIREMENT AND BENEFITS

Building upon health care, we have a very well thought out pension and benefit system that is in place to provide security in your later years. This is something that we as Canadians have put in place to ensure that elders who have contributed are taken care of. Is it perfect? No. But it does provide some cushion and the ability for basic needs to be met.

Something else that you need to be aware of is that we have several benefits at different stages in life that will come in terms of grants or tax benefits. For instance, we have a first home buyer tax credit that allows someone to access monies put into their retirement account for a department on their first home at a tax-free rate. We also have a child tax benefit, where money will be given to help support the raising of a child, or a government protected educational savings plan that allows you to save for a child's education. These are all super important, and only a small example of what is available to you and your family to be able to maximize your savings at different stages in your life.

CHANGING YOUR FAMILY'S STORY

This is very powerful and allows you to give the gift of another citizenship to your children, which will give them a world of options. You may be giving them the gift of many of the benefits that we have discussed, but taking this action allows them to have these options and will surely give them some opportunities that may or may not have been available to you.

LIFESPAN AGAIN

I know that we have already went over this above, but I feel pretty safe to say that this is that important and should be noted again. I can't logically see how you can argue with this unless you do not value each and every day and are thankful for just being alive and well. Any amount of extra time that you are able to share with yourself, your family, or in this world that we live in is a blessing, and you should be looking at any way possible to maximize it.

SOME MORE TO CONSIDER

MISSING AN OPPORTUNITY

I have seen people who have had the chance to come here and not take it. They have the option to come to Canada and they felt that they did not want it or were very "relaxed" in their approach. Those same people ended up coming back many years later, this time with more urgency, only to find that they no longer had to the option either due to a change in the law, their age, or they found that their pathway was quite a bit more complex and thus more expensive. I never try to pressure people to make a choice as I hate when I am pressured into a decision, especially for something as monumental as moving to another country. But I truly am saddened to see over the years people lose such a great opportunity for themselves and their family.

NOT HAVING A SECOND PASSPORT OR FALLBACK OPTION

Having a second passport is, for some, a very real and common goal. I generally see this for people who are confronted with security concerns and who are looking for the benefit of their future generations, as they fear some type of situation in their homeland. For others who are living in a stable environment (usually in the Western first world), they do not pay much mind to this and frankly I find this to be a huge mistake. I see a jump in applications and inquiries immediately when there is some sort of civil strife on the planet (currently Hong Kong, but also after the US election and when Crimea was annexed from the Ukraine). This has led me to believe that this is all tied into that "level two" of security that Maslow spoke of. Having another option is something I think we should all think about, as most recently it was stated to me that Venezuela used to be a great place to live but now it's not. Think about all of those people who maintained and had that second option, how much better off they would be. This is something that we should all consider, because there has been a shift in this world, and it could not only impact us but our future generations to come.

So again, thank you for being here on this journey with me. I know, that by finding this resource, you have most likely spent hours online reading different views, some positive and some negative, and others that are very misguided. I do appreciate you giving me an opportunity to help to educate you based on my experience, and I truly hope that you will benefit from my vast experience in this area. I look forward to seeing you here in Canada soon, living the life that you have dreamed, under the safety and security of the Canadian maple leaf.

CHAPTER 2:

WHY WE DO WHAT WE DO

I am going to tell you a bit of a story. It's a personal story, and something that I want to share with you, not because I want to bore you or pay homage to myself, but I feel it's important for you to understand how I have been able to build a dedicated team of immigration professionals under *Maple Immigration Service* over the course of a decade, which has allowed us to impact thousands of lives for our clients and their families. I have gotten to the point of being able to serve my clients through their Canadian immigration journey, as my past experience has provided me great insight. Because of my experience, I can empathize and understand what you are going through and what you will need, maybe even before you know it.

Immigration advising is a profession that I would never have guessed would have existed when I started out early in my career, let alone thought I would be working in. In fact, I always dreamed of becoming a lawyer. Growing up, my favourite shows were bad courtroom shows and Matlock and, truth be told, I still love those really bad courtroom shows to this day.

So, I went through school from a very young age with an interest in law and had my sights set on becoming a lawyer. After completing secondary school, I went to Carleton University, which, at the time, had the only undergraduate law program in the country, and I wanted to set myself up early for law school. However, after being well into the program and much to my chagrin, I found that law was not what I had dreamed. I was lost. Everything that I thought law was, was actually not at all what I had imagined, and there was a lot that I did not like, especially when I started to meet some members of the legal profession and when I asked myself if this is what I wanted to surround myself with.[1]

This set me on course of trying to find out what I should be doing with my life. I was very lucky that I had a supportive family that allowed me to explore. While going to school, I worked in some pretty cool jobs such as a security guard, an armed guard for a money transport company, a ramp worker at the airport, and a very junior aid to a senator.

None of these scratched an itch, and I did what many fresh grad's may or may not do, and that was turn down some pretty good job offers to find myself overseas teaching English in Korea. And guess what? This put me on a trajectory that set me up for where I am today. The plan was that I was going to go for a year, do some travel, and then come back and go to law school and become that lawyer anyway, as that was what I thought I had to do, right? *Wrong!*

So, there I was, in Korea after ten days of the idea entering my head, having sold my car, subletting my apartment, moving from Ottawa to Toronto to store my stuff, and saying goodbye to my family and friends. Oh wow, talk about a whirlwind. I recall sitting outside at the old Kimpo airport in Seoul and thinking *"Holy Cow, I'm actually here."* Truth be told the only thing that I recognised was the Coca-Cola sign and the logo of the Korean Air airplane that I just got off of. As I sat there, I was asking myself, *"What the heck am I doing here?"* Either way, I resigned myself to make a good go of it, and just proceed ahead with an open mind. I am so glad that I made this promise and followed through, as the fascinating world of Asia opened up to me

---

1   I know that is a broad brush to paint lawyers with and I apologize to my many lawyer friends/colleagues for even making this comment, but I had more than a few moments that reinforced this at that time in my life.

and changed me forever. I was so fascinated with the culture and the history that I ended up staying in Korea for more than four years.

Looking back on it today, I now realize that this key decision set me up to be able to service and understand my clients in very unique ways, no matter what area of the globe they came from. My fascination with the uniqueness of Korea scratched that explorer itch and, unbeknownst to me, allowed me to develop some very unique skills, such as an understanding and openness of different cultures, learning how to communicate within different value systems with or without language barriers, and just cultivating the open, non-judgemental mind that I have today. These are all valuable building blocks that I use every day in my business, which allows me to serve people from every corner of the world.

Teaching English was fun for a while, but I wanted to strive for more than being excellent at *Scrabble*. I learned something else, and that was that I wanted to start and run a business. So, it began with no formal training, except what I learned by starting up in the marketplace and *"learning directly with the check writers"* as one of my mentors likes to say. I do not intend on going into this sorted tale of my foray into entrepreneurialism, as this is surely another book in itself, but it is fair to say that twenty years of running businesses added to my unique skillset that has allowed me to understand how to service clients and create unique and well-thought-out client journeys.

After working in Korea and establishing my business, I came home to Toronto, Canada to live and work, with frequent trips back and forth to Asia. While working and travelling around Asia, I found that I really enjoyed my time in the Philippines (mostly as I was an avid scuba diver at that time), and really felt at home with this area of the world, the hustle and bustle, and most of all the warmth of the Filipino people.

To this end, I decided to pick up and move to the Philippines and run my business from there, as I was spending so much time being up at night in Toronto due to the time differences with Asia, and also with my frequent trips back and forth, so it only made sense. So, there I was, on another leg of my international journey, and one that was going to have the most impact on me in a way that I would have never imagined. I ended up staying there for eight years while running my core education-related business and entering into a number of other businesses with varied levels of success.

What does this all have to do with your immigrating to Canada? Well, let me tell you. I learned some valuable things about myself and laid a foundation for the second stage of my life, which was going to be nothing that I had ever dreamed of. Also, a lot of the experiences that I had and the travel I undertook allowed me to become the person that I am today, which has allowed me to produce a value system and a way of running my business to service my clients at a level that I am proud of. I have been given everything that I need to make a positive and life-changing impact on people's futures.

Value is everything that I am driven to provide in everything that I do, and I have taken some time to summarize some of the value lessons with the biggest impact that I really want to share with you. It is my hope that you will understand how these experiences have translated into me being able to bring you this book today, and why I am sought-after to provide professional immigration solutions to people such as you.

REAL LIFE BUSINESS EXPERIENCE THAT NO SCHOOL CAN TEACH

I had one of the most cutthroat, winner-take-all partners who was extremely smart, but also quite ruthless looking back at it. This always sat uneasy because, what I saw time and time again, was that we created a very unhealthy relationship with the people we worked with, since we entered into a situation that was not win-win for anyone. In fact, we were great at setting ourselves up for a toxic relationship right from the beginning.

Our team would always get the best deal, but the other side always spent their time trying to find ways to supplement the horrible arrangement, as opposed to being focused and jointly bringing value to our stated goal. This taught me a valuable lesson, and that was that no matter if I am dealing with a client, a member of my team, or a strategic partner, I always look at what value I can bring and what value I can give so that it is a good deal for them, and then I work from there. I have already spoken about the value of coming to Canada and also will speak about the value of representation, but I believe that this man's purpose was always to keep in mind that I need to create value for people that I serve.

I found that I was not happy with what I was doing. I was doing OK money-wise, and was building some businesses, but looking back, I was not really excited about it and I was looking for something else. I know it sounds cliché, but for real, you need to be happy with what you are doing, And I believe that this only becomes truly clear when you get a little older, or at least this was the case for me.

I was able to find my career in immigration by chance. It's funny when you put something out into the universe (something I firmly believe, as they say you get what you ask for). I did an education contract with a company that also had an immigration leg to them. When I found out that they were sending people to Canada, I was immediately interested and started poking around to find out more. What was interesting was that, as I started speaking to them and finding out more, I kept asking myself – *"Hmm, is that legal?"* as I knew it was certainly not moral. Upon looking into it further and asking questions, I found out that I was working with the occupational arm of a large immigration *Ghost Consultant*. I had no idea what that was at the time and will explain it later in this book. The interesting part was that, upon asking these questions and looking into it, I discovered that this whole profession existed and I got excited because I saw a way to parlay my overseas and cultural abilities, into my interest in law, while being able to help and serve to make a positive impact. This got me *very* excited and set me up to follow through on where I am today.

I MET MY BEAUTIFUL WIFE AND WE HAD OUR FIRST DAUGHTER

After spending so much time in the Philippines, I met the love of my life – Ilien. I knew that she was the one for me because, after the first day I met her, I was never apart from her and never wanted to be. Even after having a good friend visit me and after two weeks of being with Ilien, I told him that this was going to be the woman that I was going to marry, and needless to say, it raised a lot of eyebrows, but it came to fruition and I could not be happier.

So, what does this have to do with immigration? Well it has everything to do with it. I know first-hand through my experiences of sponsoring my wife, the frustrations and sleepless nights that come with this. I also understand the desire to settle in Canada, the need to have a safe place for a family. This really became apparent after the birth of my first daughter, Samantha, who I wanted to grow up in a safe environment. For me, we lived very comfortably in the Philippines, however there was not even close to the level of safety outside of our highly secure and gated community that we could enjoy in Canada, and this was at the forefront of everything that I thought when I started my journey back to Canada. This is the exact reason that people want to come here, and I understand it, as I was confronted with this as well.

This is a side note, but I lived and travelled in the Middle East and I was there right at the beginning of the Arab Spring, and I witnessed first-hand the breakdown that would domino into a lot of the instability that we see in the world today. While this was all going on, I watched with amazement, but I knew that if and when things would get out of control, I always had an escape.

This really impressed upon me how lucky I was to have that Canadian passport in my pocket, as no matter what happened or what insecurity or problem would come, I knew that for me, I could always get on the plane and escape to the safety of Canada. I also know how extremely blessed and lucky I am to have this ability; I understand how much safety and comfort this option brings to me.

PEOPLE ARE THE SAME THE WORLD OVER

After travelling and living around the world, and after countless conversations with clients, I have seen that people want nothing more than to live their lives in a peaceful and happy environment. If they are younger, they are looking for job prospects, but if they have a family or are thinking about having a family, and this is top of mind, then it all becomes about having a safe environment for their children. If you care to test this theory, go to a lively, local restaurant in any country of the world, and you will see people who are laughing and enjoying their time over a meal during a family affair. You can witness first-hand the unfettered joy and comfort they have being in safe and secure environment with family, even if it is just over that meal or family gathering.

THE VALUE OF A PESO

I always use the peso as the example because, in most of the world, the peso is less than the dollar, and when they translate, they can be quite a lot. When I lived in the Philippines, I got to understand very well how hard people work to get through life. I have always worked hard, and yes, was lucky enough to have a comfortable upbringing as well, but I have never gotten lost in the fact that I am asking for a lot of money for my services in relation to some people's budgeting but I do not ask for this lightly. I know that I *must* produce because I know exactly how hard that person has worked for their money. To me, that is OK, because when they come to Canada, they will make this money back 1000-fold, but if they do not, then they are left with quite a hole. This has always driven me to produce and only work with people that I can provide results for as I never want to leave people in a worse spot than they were in and this is what drives me to work hard to produce the desired results for my clients.

BEING THE STEWARD OF A DREAM

The dream that so many people have to come overseas has been with some them in some cases for a long time, as long as childhood in some cases when they longed to escape, felt that they did not belong, or just wanted to have a better life. Again, my time in the Philippines taught me this as well. I also know that stealing someone's dream, or killing it, is worse than any money they will pay. This is why I have made it a point to make sure that, for whoever I'm working with, I believe that I can make their dream or hopes of living a safe and secure life in Canada a reality. I will never fill people with false hope to make money, as this is tantamount to "criminal" in my mind, and anyone that knows me knows that I am actually the opposite, as I really tell it like it is. I know that I am doing a good job because some of my best referrals have come from people who I have NOT worked with, just from people who referred them because their friend said, *"At least you know with Brandon that he is going to tell it like it is and he is going to be honest with you."*

With that said, there are many who are not like me, both legal and illegal representatives. These people are only focused on extracting as much money as they can by promising that they can make it happen. What's worse than stealing anyone's money is stealing the dreams that people believe in so much, so it is incumbent on me to tell them their *exact* situation at all times. On the flip side of this, for me there is nothing more powerful than being part of making a client's dream come true for them and their family.

WE ALL HAVE OUR OWN JOURNEYS

We are all on our own journeys, and whether it is an immigration journey, or a journey to get something or another, it is always the same. I have had different journeys through my life (we all have as life it made up of these little journey's) and for me, my biggest journey that I struggle with has been my weight. I have gone from being a chunky kid and going into my twenties to earning two black belts and being in the best shape of my life to really putting on weight when I was older. I see this journey as something that I needed guidance and help with, to get to where I needed to be. This is the same service that I provide to my clients in a certain way, as a guide in their journey to Canada the same way that people have guided me in nutrition, strength training and martial arts. I do appreciate the efforts of people, such as much wife, my trainer Stefano, and my dear friends Mike and Gary, who served as guides on my journey the same way that I am guiding other people. We all have goals and aspirations and we need people to show us the best way on the pathway to that end goal.

MY LIFE AS A SCORECARD

I see my life as a scorecard, and this is why I enjoy funerals, as they are the ultimate scorecard on life. For me and my partner in life and in the business, our greatest reward is not the money, it is helping people, and the feeling we get when they come in and breathe out that sigh of relief as they have that feeling that they are well-sorted with us. They have given us their trust, and we value this above all else. The reason that I bring up funerals is not to be morbid, but I find it interesting to see how people have lived their life, and all of the kind and wonderful things they did with their time on this earth. I see my funeral (we know that it always will come) or I hope to see my funeral filled with many people with whom I have helped to positively impact their lives and change their lives forever. Whatever my funeral will look like (honestly, I won't care because I will have passed), I know that for each person I help to settle peacefully in Canada, there is another chair at my funeral that is filled with a well-wisher. This to be is what life is all about, it is not about how much wealth I can amass by moving to the top on the backs of others but in fact how many people I can impact and truly have life altering positive benefit for them and their families.

MY CLIENTS ARE MY HEROES

I am so blessed that many people see me as their hero, as I was able to help them make their Canadian dream come true, something that I am forever thankful and humbled by. However, I always remind them that, although I am very appreciative of this praise, it is a little misguided and that they should be the ones to take the credit. I was not the one that undertook this journey, but it is them who did it. I merely played a role in the bigger future that they had chosen. They were the ones who took action and did it, not me, I just served a leader role and guided them along their journey.

SO, WHAT DOES IT ALL MEAN?

It means that I have created a company that is built from all of these experiences, and I want to provide value to people who want me to work for them. It is the very reason that I am able to write this book with confidence and provide you the information you need.

I would like to point out the words that are in the logo of my company, as they form the basis for which my company, *Maple Immigration Services, has been built: trust, expertise, personalized service.* To me, these are the ultimate messages that we want to provide. What I mean by this is that, I always seek to get and gain the *trust* of my clients, and we provide valuable service and advice through our *expertise.* Because immigration and the matters that we are dealing with are very unique, we aim to provide *personalized service,* as everyone's circumstances are different, and they need tailored services to meet their needs and goals.

Looking back, I think a lot about some of the important lessons, and today they are even more pronounced as they really have been woven into every facet of my business for me and for each member of my team. I promised you that this chapter was not about paying homage to me, but it was about impressing upon you the values that I hold dear, in order to be able to serve my clients. I firmly believe that it is for this very reason that I have enjoyed so much success with *Maple Immigration Services,* and these lessons are why we are going to be able to continue to grow as an organization to provide value and to positively impact so many people's lives, while serving you our client with services that will positively impact your life for years to come.

CHAPTER 3 :

A HOLISTIC APPROACH TO CANADIAN IMMIGRATION

Whenever I speak to anyone about immigration, they are more often than not surprised when I tell them that getting permanent residence is the easy part, and the hard part is settling into Canada and knowing how to best use their skills. Some will shrug this off with disbelief, and it is not usually until later that they will come to find that this is the truth.

I see the steps to success in anything that we need to do as the same, no matter what we choose to undertake. We need to have a clearly defined plan and also a way to execute on that plan, as otherwise, no matter how good the plan may be, it is only a dream. Dreams are great, but without a way to execute them, they only remain just that.

I know that you understand this. If you look back over your life, you have had to plan and take action to get to where you are now, and you know that you have always had to take the time to invest yourself in a process to get what you want done properly. Immigration to Canada is no different. I always ask people to take a step back and look at the whole process in a bird's eye view. I did this when I created a system, we call *The Immigration Success System*™, is the secret formula for all of the success that we have been able to pass on to our clients over the years.

Before I dive into this system, I would like to draw your attention to something that I was lucky to learn very early in my immigration career. This is where a large number of people make their biggest mistakes. Simply, people are too focused on getting here. They do not take into account or fully grasp how to integrate and translate their skills into Canada. This is a huge mistake made by a number of people where they think that just getting here is the end of the journey.

This was not only an observation for me, but while transitioning into the immigration field, I was lucky to be hired by a company to help people learn how to settle into Canada effectively. This opened my eyes to this difficult struggle, hence the reason that I highlight this to clients very early on in the process. I was lucky, as I was able to effectively help a number of people get off to the best start, they could have here in Canada, with better than average jobs, while teaching them how to effectively navigate their newfound home.

I will be speaking a lot more about this in later chapters, but this is what I refer to when I talk about a "Holistic Process". *The Immigration Success System* ™ has three stages and eight steps. This process has been developed after many years of understanding and observing where clients will struggle and how people have gone off track. This process is key to fundamentally guiding people to properly execute everything they have to do in the time that they need to, so as not to have to pay the ultimate price of sacrificing their opportunity to immigrate to Canada.

STAGE 1: PLANNING

This stage is the most important part of the process and this is the starting point for anyone who wishes to work with me and the Maple Immigration team. This is the formulation of the plan which sets you up for success.

Any professional will understand the importance of this, and I always use countless examples to try and hit this point home when I speak with people. This is the importance of a professional assessment. One of my favorite examples of this is when you go to the doctor's office. You don't usually come in and tell the doctor that you are sick and suggest a cure or prescription to the doctor. What generally tends to happen, is that the doctor will ask you a series of questions, possibly proceed to run some tests, and then put you through a funnel which will then lead to a diagnosis and a solution/treatment plan.

This is similar to doing an assessment, as your goal is to get a solution or a "script" in this case, which will lead to your Canadian immigration cure. You cannot proceed unless you know your options, or in the case above, what ails you. You need to proceed professionally and understand your cure, so that you can get what is required in order to continue ahead properly and professionally.

To underscore this and give you some context about some *very* real situations I am confronted with, I sometimes will have a prospective client that will come to me in their initial call, telling me what they qualify for and how they wish to proceed in this manner. I tend to listen and let them explain, and then I am very quick to remind them that there are ninety or more pathways to immigration, with different variations, and they are only looking through a small hole at one option that they think works for them. This is not always a bad thing however, because one thing that I am always looking for as a success criteria is someone who is "coachable" (i.e., will take direction and let us take the lead in their future, while at the same time someone who is engaged in the process and understands their own situation).

I find that these types of clients need an immediate reset. What may have worked for their friend or what they may have read online might be different from what they need, and they must take a personalized approach to their own situation.

It is important that you understand what options are available to you and how to work them to your advantage. This stage is broken down into two steps of my process.

STEP 1: THE DISCOVERY SESSION™

As a professional, when I am at this stage, I'm putting the client through a funnel that will determine the programs they will qualify for, the options that are available to them, and the quickest way through the immigration system for their unique situation, all while being mindful of the most cost effective and safest pathways for them and their family.

On top of that, I have a professional obligation to do all of these things and ensure that I make all of these things happen for my clients, while also making sure that I do not waste their money or their time. This is something that we treat very seriously. It is also important to determine if there are any "deal breakers" or things that need to be managed so that the plan can be formulated for the client. I call these proclivities the "by the ways." I will be sure to explain this more when we talk about inadmissibility in a subsequent chapter.

After going through a systematic discovery session and understanding what options are best suited to your personalized situation, and also by discovering any possibly impediments, we will proceed to the second and final step of this first stage.

STEP 2: THE IMMIGRATION BLUEPRINT™

As you now know from the first step, we need to gather the information and then put it all together into a workable and executable immigration plan, which will form the basis for executing on the next stage – processing your application. This is the step where all of your personalized information that has been collected and has been worked through, will then be put together and all of your options will be laid out.

You will understand the pros and cons to each immigration pathway, as well as the timeframes and how they will relate to your timing to settle in Canada. This step will also include anything that you need to be aware of and if there are any issues. You will need to understand how these issues should be presented, and what is relevant to be given to the immigration officer who will ultimately be deciding your fate.

The end result will be to have the plan in place that will set you up for success, not only with the second stage, but with your ultimate goal which is to immigrate and settle in Canada.

STAGE 2: IMPLEMENTATION

This is arguably one of the most exciting, but also one of the most nerve-wracking, sections of the process. The reason being is that this is where it all happens and where you get to hop on that The *Immigration Roller Coaster*™ I always use the term "roller coaster" as this really can describe the ride with all of the ups and downs that come with this process. It can either be a fun ride or one that scares the heck out of you.

Imagine being on a roller coaster where you never know where the highs and lows are, and you will never know when you are going to be thrown into a loop. Well, this is what can happen if you are not prepared, not advised, or educated. But if you know what the ride will look like, then you will have a much better experience. This is why Stage 1 is so fundamental and so important. So now that we are on this ride, we have divided this into three distinct phases, collecting/

putting together the application, submitting to the government, and processing the finalization to land in Canada.

STEP 3: THE APPLICATION BUILD™

Collecting documentation and moving through the building of your file is the start Implementing the plan or *"Making it Happen"*. This is a daunting process and it can be filled with many pitfalls, most of which are not readily apparent to the layman until they are confronted at a later stage. It is imperative that you put this together and are as comprehensive as possible, as this will set the tone for what will happen while you are processing your file with the government and will determine the type ride that you will go on during the immigration processing journey.

STEP 4: THE TACTICAL SUBMISSION™

After you have put together a comprehensive file, it will be submitted to the immigration department for processing. This is the area of the process that we refer to as the *"black hole,"* as things will disappear into the department. You will be confronted with a lot of late nights, wondering what is happening, with a lot of worry and second guessing when, in fact, if things are done correctly, you have nothing to worry about. This is quite normal, and it is truly at this point when my clients truly being to understand the value of having a professional work on their file as they have someone to call and get some context to their situation. This is not to say that things don't fall off the rails due to errors by the department (I can assure you that I have fixed many of them over the years and at the time of writing this book I am dealing with two very serious department transgressions), but under normal circumstances, if you have effectively planned and submitted a strong application, then it is just a waiting and reacting game at this point, and you will have to be calculating in how you will deal with any requests.

STEP 5: THE LANDING EXPERIENCE™

This is the last stage of processing stage and should be the victory lap of the Implementation Stage. Assuming that all has gone well, this phase will conclude with you and your family transitioning to Canada successfully and confidently to start your new life. Even though you are through this phase, there is still work to be done, and there are things that you will still need to be aware of right up until that time that you have landed and been a confirmed PR (Permanent Resident) in Canada (a day that you have waited for, for a long time after many restless wondering nights). This is one of the happiest days for the vast majority of people, but I have seen a few cases over the years where this assumed happiest day has turned into a nightmare for some who made some critical errors and lost their chance to come to Canada at the airport on their landing day. You must be sure to not lose focus nor take anything for granted at this stage until you are landed and safely in Canada as a permanent resident.

STAGE 3: SETTLEMENT

This is the most important and often most overlooked part of the process, something that I said at the start of this chapter and you will probably hear me say over and over and for good reason. Many people have the intention to settle in Canada, and they engage the services of a professional to get them there or to figure out ways to make sure it happens. But then, when they arrive, they are lost and are not able to maximize their skills by translating them into the Canadian context. This is a major oversight and can lead to the Canadian dream caving in, if they do not treat this seriously.

From my time of working with newcomers and looking at options and ways to effectively settle in and use their skills on the ground, I developed two distinct steps in my process which include pre-settlement planning, and settlement into Canada.

STEP 6: THE PRE-SETTLEMENT FORMULA™

This is a very individualized stage, and this will not only encompass the principal applicant to the process, but also look at aspects of settlement for the rest of the family into Canada. This step should start prior to the approval of the immigration application, and will vary in complexity depending on your situation, and the landing time into Canada. Most people don't know that they can be working to get their stuff taken care of and completed prior to leaving their home country. This is integral to setting themselves up for success. This stage is a distinct plan that you will use to be able to settle and know exactly where you are going to go and how you will get there.

STEP 7: THE SETTLEMENT ADVANTAGE™

You are now in Canada, and through the work that you did in your pre-settlement planning, you are executing on your plan and settling in properly. You may have hit a few bumps along the way, but these are minor, as you have a plan in place and have taken these into account, especially due to your knowledge and understanding of your new home.

STEP 8: THE CITIZENSHIP SOLUTION™

This is the last phase of the journey to immigrate and settle in Canada. Canadian citizenship allows you to call Canada your true home where no one can deny you the right to enter while giving you all the rights and protections that this coveted status entails. This is the last stage in their immigration journey that has lasted years and has culminated in your achieving this major milestone in life.

A FINAL WORD

Now that you have arrived in Canada and have settled in, you have achieved a huge life-changing goal. You will have the option at a later date to receive your Canadian citizenship, and this is actually something that you might want to consider for a number of different reasons. Should you decide that Canadian citizenship is for you, this would *really* complete your immigration journey with the immigration department once and for all, but this is a whole different topic and one that will be last and will come later, should you wish to take this option.

I look forward to expanding all of these steps in my process for you in later chapters, where we will do a deep dive into these areas and explore what you need to be doing at each stage to ensure that you are prepared and are able to execute on your immigration goals.

CHAPTER 4:

THE DISCOVERY SESSION™

I hope that at this point you understand the importance of assessing yourself and that you realize the importance that this holds for your immigration future. It provides you with the basis for a roadmap on how to best proceed with a good understanding of the questions you should be asking, both for yourself, and for people who may work with you along this journey that you are about to embark upon.

The overall theme of this chapter is planning, and this is the first stage of the process that has been the basis for countless successful applications that I have overseen and facilitated. Planning is the key to a successful immigration application, but you already understand this as this is why you are taking the time to read this book. Congratulations to you, because believe it or not, you are one of a small group of people that plan ahead and do the research necessary to be successful in their immigration and settlement aspirations in Canada.

Planning an immigration application is no different from anything that you do in life, in that you need to understand how you will be able to get what you want and what the best approach is to that stated goal of immigration to Canada, so that you can find a safe and secure place for your family. I don't have to tell you this, as you have already achieved so much in life and you know that planning and execution are key variables to any successful undertaking.

So now that we all agree that planning is fundamental, I would like to set the stage for this chapter and explain some important elements with respect to planning that I will cover in this section:

- What an immigration assessment is and what it isn't.

- Elements of the assessment and areas that a professional will look at in the assessment.

- An overview of the immigration system and some key programs as they relate to the assessment.

- Deciding if you are going to self-represent or if you should use a professional.

- What are your options for professionals, and what type of professional should you use?

- What is the value of having a professional represent your application?

- The different types of inadmissibility and how they can impact you.

WHAT AN IMMIGRATION ASSESSMENT IS & WHAT IT ISN'T

The assessment procedure that we employ at Maple Immigration, which is conducted either by myself or another professional, is very robust. Done properly, this should take at the very minimum an hour of interview time, just to gather and confirm the details. It explores all aspects of the prospective client's personal history, family history, education history, language ability, employment history, immigration/travel history, and other areas that might be pertinent due to the persons unique situations.

Over the years, I have developed an assessment procedure that we use which is a funnel and has proven to be flawless. I built a standardized assessment model that ensures that we systematically go through all areas of immigration options and use this to effectively plan for the client. This is truly a unique approach, and one that not only sets us apart from others, but also lays the foundation for our client's success.

So now that you know briefly what an assessment is, let me tell you what it is not and what you need to be careful of. There are countless people out there who are offering fifteen-minute free consultations, and this is just wrong on so many levels, as it is not possible to come up with a complete plan or do a thorough assessment of your situation in this amount of time. If, after speaking with someone for ten or fifteen minutes, they are ready to break out in agreement and say, "you're qualified," and they're ready to press ahead – *run away*. There is no way to be able to do a thorough job or construct a thorough plan without a deeper level of understanding into your situation.

It is fine to have a discussion with a professional and ask some questions, but most busy and seasoned professionals will be quite measured in their responses and details as it relates to your situation, due to professional liability issues, by giving out specific legal advice. Personally, I believe that we have found a happy medium in our process, as prior to having the person do a *"discovery session"* with us, we have them invest their time and do a quick ten-minute free, online assessment, where the person will fill in their details and answer some key questions. By doing this, we are able to see quite quickly if a person is even able to have any type of pathway forward. We do this as a matter of courtesy to our prospective clients, because if they cannot get through this stage, there is no point for them to go to a paid session when I can tell quite quickly whether they will have a chance or not. This way, we make sure that they are not needlessly wasting their time or money for something that had a bad chance of leading anywhere.

ELEMENTS THAT A PROFESSIONAL WILL ASSESS

Depending on the program, the assessment will be dynamic. We have designed our process through a checklist that is dynamic and based on conditional logic, where if questions are answered a certain way, then other questions or groups of questions will be asked. This ensures that we do not miss anything and are open to explore more in-depth circumstances only where it applies. The sections that we discuss and the goal of each section when doing an assessment are as follows,

PERSONAL HISTORY

The goal of providing your personal history is to track what you have been doing since you were eighteen years of age. We need to know your employment history, travel history, residency history, education history, and any other type of activity, including periods of time that you were not working. The purpose behind disclosing this history is for the government to ensure that you are not a risk to public safety to Canada. This information will be used by the government to see if any additional documents may be required, such as police certificates for countries that you have lived in for more than six months since you were eighteen. We may also want to look at whether you should look further into a medical examination prior to being examined by the panel physician to see if there are any medical concerns that should be looked at and addressed prior to being scrutinized under an immigration medical.

Although most of the forms only ask you to document your personal history for the past ten years, we ask for your history going back to when you were eighteen years of age if your eighteenth birthday falls prior to the last ten years. Our reason for doing this is to ensure that we give them more than what they need so that they don't come back later and ask for more information.

The information provided in your background history can also be used to verify other aspects of your application. For example, how does your educational background match up with your employment history? This can be important, depending on the type of application being submitted. It also allows me, the consultant, to see if there are any weaknesses in your application that need to be addressed. For example, you are applying for a study permit to take a post-graduate course in a field that you have no background in, but you have been employed in that field abroad. This information will be used to argue why pursuing this type of study in Canada is relevant to you, based on your background activities.

This is also why it is so important to not leave any gaps in your personal history. Your personal history helps me to paint an overall picture of you.

FAMILY HISTORY/DETAILS

The purpose of providing your immediate family history is also one concerned with the safety and security of Canada, as it allows the government to run background checks of your family members. This is especially important for any immigration programs to which you are applying for that could allow you to sponsor an eligible dependent at the time of your application, or for a dependent you may wish to sponsor in the future.

It is very important that you declare all of your family members as required. Any dependent family members you declare, whether you plan to bring them with you now or in the future, will also have background checks run by the immigration department. This may include police checks and medical examinations. Not declaring your dependents can lead to a refusal of your application or losing your ability to sponsor a dependent family member in the future. The government will also look at admissibility of your family members to see if you are admissible to Canada. For example, if one of your family members has serious criminality issues or serious medical issues, you may be found to be inadmissible to Canada because of this.

In cases where you have family members living in Canada as either PRs or citizens, this information will help show your ability to adapt to life in Canada and it may even open up certain pathways, such as provincial nomination programs, that look for your ties to the province.

EDUCATION HISTORY

Declaring your education history is important, as it is one tool that the immigration department will use to evaluate your skill sets and whether you would be a good fit to immigrate to Canada. The government is committed to attracting highly skilled workers to meet shortfalls in our labour market. Knowing your complete educational background allows us to see what immigration programs you may be eligible for and what the best possible pathway might be for you. This is especially true for the economic programs leading to permanent residence. For example, the higher your education, the more points you will be assessed for in the *Express Entry*[2] application system.

Providing your full education history, including secondary school, post-secondary, and trade or apprenticeship certificates is important in helping to see what pathways are best for you. It also allows us to see if your educational background can be updated by pursuing additional studies in Canada, which could open up new pathways to PR that were previously not available to you.

It also allows us to help evaluate your education against the Canadian system to see if you have education equivalencies to programs in Canada or, again, if upgrading your skills could help open up new pathways for you.

LANGUAGE ABILITY

This area is very important when dealing with economic grouped programs. Canada will always look at language ability because studies have shown that a proven indicator of the ability for a prospective immigrate to get off to a great start in Canada is their language ability. When dealing with family-type programs, such as sponsoring a spouse or a child, this does not need to be assessed, but this is truly an important factor for most areas of immigration assessment.

EMPLOYMENT HISTORY

---

2   Express Entry is an application system that is used by the immigration department to accept applications under 4 different programs which are the FSW (Federal Skilled Worker), CEC (Canadian Experience Class), FSTP (Federal Skilled Trades Program) and PNP (Provincial Nominee Programs)

Canada is committed to attracting skilled workers and meeting identified labour and economic shortfalls. Knowing your full employment history helps to verify your qualifications and skills and to see if you are a good fit for the Canadian economy.

Your foreign work experience, including the type of skilled work you have done, is important in determining if you qualify for a number of economic programs, such as the foreign skilled worker or trades person streams. Any supporting documents you have for your foreign work history are important to include in your application, as a way for the immigration department to evaluate and verify your work history. This includes letters from your current and former employers, employment contracts, tax statements, pay statements, and any foreign certificates you have been awarded. This allows the government to assess your work qualifications against Canadian standards.

Any work experience you have in Canada, either presently or within the past three years, is also important to identify because again, it could open up other pathways to PR for you. With Express Entry, you are issued additional points for each year of work you completed in Canada, as long as it was or is evaluated as skilled work. Your job duties are very important, as they allow the government to see how your work experience relates to the NOC[3] which is a system that the government uses to assess the skill level of the job for immigration programs amongst other things important to the labor market in Canada.

Your work history is also important to see if you qualify for other short-term programs, that may lead to permanent residency (such as caregiver pilot projects). Or, to see if your work experience can be used to help you enter the student pathway where your education background might not meet criteria for admission to a particular program at a Canadian post-secondary institution and provide you not only with a pathway to immigration but give you a head-start on settling into Canada.

---

3   The NOC is an acronym that stands for the National Occupational Classification. This is a system that we use to classify all types of jobs in Canada and is key to an economic type application. It is made up of a 4-digit number that can easily show such things as the industry and skill level of any job in Canada.

It's also very important to know periods of your life where you were unemployed, as we would want to address why you were not employed to avoid additional questions from the immigration department. For example, many people commit to their families and cannot work for extended periods of time because they are taking care of loved ones and are not able to work.

FINANCIAL RESOURCES

Your financial resources are important, as it demonstrates your ability to support yourself and/or your family members. Depending on the program, the government will assess your finances to ensure that you will not end up relying on government assistance once you become a permanent resident.

You are also required to show financial resources to support temporary visas to come to Canada, and this is especially true for international students wanting to study here. We ask about your net worth, your personal savings, assets, holdings, and your ability to access any of your investments. If you are applying for a study permit and have co-sponsors, we will also want to see their financial records to see and demonstrate that they are capable of providing support to you as well. In addition to this, we will ask for letters and documents from your employer and your financial supporters' employers to show where your income is coming from. Your tax returns are also important documents that help to verify your access to funds. Financial resources are particularly important for foreign students – the cost of education for an international student in Canada is about $25,000 to $30,000 per year, including tuition and living expenses, and in our experience, sometimes the amount of investment in a student's future is overlooked.

Your available financial resources are important for some immigration programs, as you may be required to show settlement funds in order to be approved for permanent residence. Your total net worth and assets can also open up certain immigration programs, depending on the amount of funds available to you under certain business/investment programs. They also play an important role for a visitor visa (which we call in Canada a TRV[4]), as they would like to know that you can support your travels here.

It is important to establish that you have access to funds, either through yourself, family members, or employers/friends. I hope after reading this section that you understand how just this one factor can have some much impact on many different types of immigration applications from the simple to complex, and for temporary to permanent programs. It is important to understand the nuances of finances with respect to the particular program that you are applying for and how these should be presented to maximize your chances of a positive result by the decision maker.

IMMIGRATION/TRAVEL HISTORY

One of the most important criteria used to evaluate admissibility to Canada, whether for a temporary or permanent purpose, is your immigration and travel history. Including this information is very important so that background checks can be made for security and safety purposes.

Arguably more important for temporary residence, the government will want to know if you have always abided by any previous immigration status given to you. It is important to know all of the countries you have previously resided in or visited, and also that you met the terms of any temporary status you held, so the impact on the given application can be measured. We also want to know if you are, or have applied to be, a permanent resident of any other country, as it goes toward showing your intent to permanently reside in Canada. For example, if you have applied for a green card in the US and are applying for permanent residence in Canada, this can raise a red flag with the immigration department if not presented properly, as they will question your objectives to immigrate and stay in Canada. As immigration professionals, we need to know this information so that we can address it in your application. In other words, we can identify

---

4   A TRV stands for a Temporary Resident Visa which is commonly known as a Visitor Visa. The TRV is the sticker that is placed in your passport prior to travel to Canada. This allows you to travel to Canada and present yourself for examination to a CBSA (Canadian Border Services Agency) Officer. It is important to know that not everyone requires a TRV and only people from certain countries will require this.

it as a weakness in a potential application and address it head on and frame it with the hope that the immigration officer will be satisfied with the provided explanation in the application.

Knowing your current and past immigration status and travel history goes toward showing that an applicant has always respected terms of their past visas, especially when applying for temporary permits to come to Canada. If a client has no travel history, this is something we will want to know as well, as we will need to address this and explain why there was no travel history. Not having travel history is often a reason used by officers to deny a temporary permit to an applicant.

Knowing your past history in Canada will also help us to better decide which pathway may be best suited to you and allow us to construct your best immigration plan.

OVERVIEW OF THE IMMIGRATION SYSTEM & KEY PROGRAMS

The Canadian Immigration system can be broken down into a number of different categories. For the purpose of this chapter, I think it would be best to highlight the most common pathways to permanent residence, and how they should be looked at with respect to the bona fides of the pathway and how to properly assess yourself in this category.

ECONOMIC PROGRAMS

Goals and objectives behind the economic programs are to address labor shortages in Canada and to attract talented and skilled foreigners to address those needs. Canada identifies specific skill shortages and labor shortages throughout the country, and tries to address these through the various economic classes. We want to address specific labor shortages by specific jobs and skills, as well as being able to retain new skilled workers provincially, i.e. address specific provincial needs.

There are several economic immigration programs developed to meet these goals. Some of the more popular ones in attracting skilled workers are the Federal Skilled Workers (FSW), Federal Skilled Trades (FST), Canadian Experience Class (CEC), & Provincial Nominee Programs (PNP).

One of the most important aspects of the economic programs is the goal of not only attracting skilled foreign workers, but also to evaluate their ability to become economically established in Canada. We want to attract workers that will stay in Canada and contribute to growing our economy and making us competitive in the world market, while achieving economic goals within the country as well.

BUSINESS PROGRAMS

There are several federal economic business immigration classes. The objectives behind the creation of these programs was to attract permanent and temporary residents that will help to strengthen Canada's economy. The government established several programs, including the Startup, Entrepreneur, and Investor classes, to select and admit business immigrants who would be able to establish themselves economically in Canada. We also want business immigrants who can create job opportunities for Canadians and share benefits of expanding economic development activities, both provincially and across the country.

Business immigration classes are aimed at promoting economic development and creating jobs in Canada by attracting business immigrants with relevant skills and capital. The goal is that these immigrants will aid in developing new commercial opportunities, improving Canadian access to foreign markets, and supporting provincial and territorial economic objectives.

THE STUDENT PATHWAY

The government of Canada wants to attract and retain international students from around the world. One of the government's goals has been to attract almost half a million international students by 2022.

This goal was achieved by the end of 2017, surpassing expectations almost five years early. Canada is a world leader in attracting international students and recently these number have only been growing while we are seeing this pathway emerge as one of the most popular pathways to permanent residence in Canada.

Canada's post-secondary education system is highly lauded throughout the international community and degrees from Canada often give students a head-start for employment. Canada has made a commitment to attracting students that can contribute to our economic, social and cultural development. One commitment to this is the Student Direct Stream, which facilitates faster processing for students applying from a few selected countries at this moment, but the immigration department is increasing the roll-out of this stream to more selected countries every day.

Not only does Canada want to attract international students, but it also wants to train and retain them with offers of pathways whereby the temporary student status can be used as a transition into permanent resident status. Canada has implemented a Post Graduate Work Permit (known as the PGWP) which further attracts international students. The PGWP allows eligible students to obtain a work permit following graduation that allows them to work in Canada for up to three years in total (depending on their program length), and gain valuable Canadian work experience, which can then help them achieve necessary experience and points to qualify for permanent residence through Express Entry system.

There are also provincial nomination programs that specifically focus on attracting students that have either studied in that province or elsewhere in Canada.

THE TEMPORARY WORKER'S PATHWAY

Millions of people visit Canada every year. This includes visitors as well as those who come to study and work on a temporary basis. There are a variety of temporary work permits that can lead to PR, and these include the already mentioned PGWP, caregiver programs, and economic programs. Most of these require at least one year of Canadian work experience in a certain skilled job category before you can be eligible to apply for PR. Again, the government is committed to growing our economy and diversity by addressing shortfalls in labor markets and skill types both across the country and on a province by province basis.

Your language ability, education, and employment background can help determine a pathway that is right for you. The minimum qualifications for each of these will vary by program. Some of these pathways require minimal settlement funds while others do not.

FAMILY PROGRAMS

The goal of the family class programs is family reunification. The federal government has referred to family reunification as a *"central pillar of Canada's immigration program that contributes to the economic, social and cultural prosperity of all Canadians."* One of the major advantages of becoming a permanent resident of Canada is the ability to potentially sponsor additional family members for PR in the future. There are currently three main family sponsorship streams within the family class of programs that exist. These include the ability to sponsor your spouse or partner, your dependent child/children, and your parents or grandparents. It may be possible to sponsor other family members, but only in very exceptional circumstances.

One of the important things to keep in mind when you commit to sponsoring a family member is that you must be willing to sign an undertaking to be responsible for the family member. This is a legal commitment to ensure that the person(s) being sponsored do not have to become a public burden whereby they will be relying on social or financial assistance from the government. An undertaking means that you will be responsible for their financial "wellbeing" for a certain number of years, depending on the type of family member you are sponsoring. In addition to proving that you are eligible to sponsor, the applicant must also be eligible for PR; they cannot be criminally inadmissible, and, in some cases, they cannot be medically inadmissible. Their family members' history can also affect the applicant's eligibility for admissibility to Canada.

Settlement funds are generally not required, but there are exceptions, as noted above, and you should be able to show that you can support the person(s) you are sponsoring. You must also establish the genuineness of the relationship, especially in the case of sponsoring your spouse or partner – this is one of the most important aspects of the application. You'll need to show that this is a real and genuine marriage/partnership, and not one that is for the purposes of immigration.

REFUGEE PROGRAMS

Refugees are not immigrants. They are people who have fled their countries because of a well-founded fear of persecution. They can't return home and have been forced to flee, often in order to save their lives.

Canada is a signatory to a number of agreements and treaties and must maintain its commitments to refugees and vulnerable persons, despite an influx of asylum seekers in the last two years that have strained the government's resources.

At Maple Immigration Services we generally do not take on refugee cases, as this is a whole different area of practice that we do not focus on. Canada is committed to protecting the world's most vulnerable people, and this is reflected in the annual budget and our international agreements that we are signatories to.

SELF-REPRESENTING VS. USING A PROFESSIONAL

Part of planning is deciding on how you are going to put together an application, and whether you will do it yourself or engage the services of a professional. This is a common dilemma that many people have. At first glance, things look quite easy, as it is all laid out on the internet – *wrong!*

Truth be told, I have a great deal of contempt for the immigration department telling you that you do not need a professional and that you can do it yourself. We are talking about immigration law after all, which is a body of law that is quite complicated and has a number of layers, which are not known to the lay person.

To make matters worse, the website and the contents of the website are *not* the law, as authority is given through the statutes that make up IRPA (The Immigration and Refugee Protection Act) and the regulations that are in place to law out how the act should be administered. On top of this, there are other materials that the common user is not aware of, which can impact the processing of applications, such as public policy, operational bulletins, and guides that are internal that have been "scrubbed" in most recent years, from public consumption. This is a myth that everything is on the internet and this could not be further from the truth, and this falsehood that is being propagated can have serious consequences if you get caught up in something that was not understood.

So to my original point, I find it somewhat irresponsible for the department to popularize the belief that people do not need representation, and that they can self-represent when they may not understand what impact this may have on their future. With the number of rules and policies that can impact a person, just one little detail may change the person's whole case and lead them down a pathway that they may not be able to come back from.

It is obvious that I make my living through providing immigration services and my views might be seen as somewhat biased and self-serving, but I can assure you that over the years I have seen people self-represent themselves into a mess. Some have dug their hole so deep that they are unable to get out of it and have destroyed their chances of being able to immigrate to Canada forever.

On the other hand, I have also seen others, "the precious few" as I call them, who have done a wonderful job and have come to me over some small hiccup they are having. In reviewing their work, but I am super impressed by how far they have gotten on their own and what they have been able to put together in terms of a professional and well-articulate application, but again, these are really only a handful that stick out to me over time.

In short, I believe that everyone should work with a professional to, at the very least, have a proper and full assessment conducted and to know where they stand and if there are any flags that they should be aware of so that they can proceed responsibly. From there, part of your planning phase should be a real heart-to-heart with yourself to determine the level of service/representation that you require in order to be able to meet your goals.

YOUR OPTIONS FOR PROFESSIONAL REPRESENTATION

When dealing with a Canadian immigration application, there are two different types of people who can represent your application for a fee, which include either a regulated immigration consultant or a lawyer who is a member of a provincial bar. With respect to a lawyer it must be noted that this does not include a lawyer who is overseas and not qualified or a Canadian lawyer. These lawyers should not be practicing Canadian law and I would venture to say are breeching their code of conduct/ethics of their local bar by doing so.

There are many opinions as to who is better, and when this conversation comes up, there tends to be a breakdown of discourse amongst the professional groups. I tend not to engage in this conversation, as I look at it that it really boils down to the individual that you are working with under this personalized process, and there are things that you need to know about what you need and the services that they can provide.[5]

WHAT IS THE VALUE OF HAVING A

---

5   As my gift to you I've outlined the differences between these two professionals. You can download an information and a worksheet to use when interviewing a prospective professional. Find this info online at www.mysecondpassport.ca/professional

PROFESSIONAL REPRESENT YOUR APPLICATION?

The value that I bring to a client's application is a leadership role, as I serve as the guide through a complicated legal process. I always know what the next step is going to be, and I proactively anticipate and plan an application strategically, and if there is an issue, I am there to respond and guide you.

Additionally, as the authorized representative on a client file, I am the point of contact for the immigration department on the file and responsible for handling all correspondence with the government while ensuring that there are proper responses. I also ensure that the government stays within their bounds with respect to the processing of my client's file and does not overstep their requests or power.

It is my job as a professional to always be educating myself, so that I can provide my clients with the most up-to-date knowledge and expertise in an ever-changing environment. This is an integral part of my value, as I know what is going on, what is normal, (or not normal) at any given time in the ever-shifting sands of Canadian immigration.

When things go wrong, I am able to get ahead of the issue and know exactly what to do, while knowing what is right and what is not right. This allows us to correct any errors made by the visa officer, while knowing how to navigate the department to raise potential issues to the appropriate power in order. That way, we can ensure that things are taken care of properly and fairly for the client.

Lastly, a common misconception that people think, is that we just fill out and assemble forms. I am very quick to correct people on this, as yes, this is a portion of the service that we provide, but this is by no means the value that we bring. Most people don't realize this until they have an issue or have a long sleepless night, wondering what is going on with their application.

I personally see myself as a nation builder who is beginning the next generation of Canadians to the country, and who will exhibit the values that make this country great.

INADMISSIBILITY

If you recall in my last chapter, I went on at length about my time in Korea and how it shaped me and what I do today. Well, in dealing with inadmissibility issues with immigration, I see these as those overlooked areas that have a good chance of being skipped over, and will be the quickest way to destroy your application. I best describe these as a "by the ways," a term that I have effectively brought forward into my assessment process from my time in Korea. Here is a great example and a real story I might add that underscores where this term came from, and one that formed a conversation that went like this. "Oh, by the way Brandon, we have a staff dinner for 200 people after school and you are expected to be there, as you will be one of the honorary guests and it starts in about forty-five minutes. Why aren't you ready, and is that what you are going to wear?"

Much to my surprise (and with my mouth no doubt gapping open) I let one of my Korean counterparts politely know that this is the first I was hearing about this and questioned how I could be expected to be ready for such an auspicious occasion. He then went on to tell me that we had been discussing it in the meeting for weeks, and that I should've known about this, to which I politely reminded my colleague that I did not speak Korean, and even though I was there I had no idea what was being discussed due to an obvious language barrier.

So how does this relate to the discovery session? Well, in finding out what is required for your unique situation, a bunch of questions need to be asked so we can avoid the "by the ways." For example, having a simple misdemeanor DUI (Driving Under the Influence) might be no big deal in some places, but currently under Canadian immigration law, this results in an inadmissibility and will result in a situation where you could be denied if you do not file your application taking this into account.

So, this is the perfect transition for me to speak about the three most common types of inadmissibility.

CRIMINAL

There are several types of criminality that may make you inadmissible to Canada. You should know that if you were convicted of an offence in Canada or out of Canada in the past, you may be inadmissible, depending on the type of crime, when it occurred, where it occurred, and if there was a conviction or not. The Canadian government is committed to protecting its citizens and carefully examines your history to ensure you are not a public danger to yourself or anyone else. There are serious crimes for which you will not be admissible to Canada. These include those related to security reasons, such as terrorism, human rights violations, and war crimes. Serious criminality includes organized crimes. Other crimes such as DUI's in the US may also render you inadmissible. The type of criminality that you have will help determine next steps and see if you can overcome it and be rehabilitated. Because the government is committed to protecting Canada and its citizens, criminal inadmissibility applies to all immigration programs.

MEDICAL

For most permanent resident applications, you and your family members must undergo a medical exam first. You may be found medically inadmissible for three reasons: you are a danger to public health, you are a danger to public safety, or your medical condition may cause excessive demand on Canada's health or social services. To be a danger to public health means that you have a health condition that could be dangerous to others because of an infectious disease that you have, or you may have been in close contact with someone that has a disease such as tuberculosis or syphilis. You may be considered a danger to public safety because your health condition may include unpredictable behavior on your part, or violent behavior. Your health condition may be considered to represent an excessive demand on Canada's health or social services if the treatment of your medical condition might negatively affect wait times for services in Canada, or the services needed would cost more than a threshold that has been established by the government, the excessive demand threshold. You should know that not all PR immigration classes are subject to medical inadmissibility, including some family sponsorship classes.

FINANCIAL

You may also be required to meet certain minimal financial criteria to be admissible to Canada. If you cannot meet financial criteria set by certain programs, you could be deemed financially inadmissible and be refused. For example, you do not meet settlement fund requirements for PR under the federal skilled worker program or the caregiver pilot programs. You must prove to the government that you are capable of supporting yourself and your family members financially, so that you do not become a burden on our social systems. In other words, if you are unable to financially support yourself or your family members accompanying you, you may be denied PR. If you are not willing to support your family members, you can also be found financially inadmissible, or if you are on social assistance, etc. you may not be admissible.

CHAPTER 5 :

THE IMMIGRATION BLUEPRINT™

Y ou've just completed your assessment and now you are at the point of putting it together to devise your plan of action which will carry you into the next phase where you will *Make it Happen.* This is your plan that you will execute for your immigration application which will maximize your chances of success and give you a road map for what that roller coaster is going to look like.

You are now fully armed with your details, and it is time to prepare to do battle with the immigration department. Prior to you launching your offensive in the form of filing an application, you need to have a fully prepared plan or attack on how you will lodge this application and how you will be victorious. This blueprint will allow you to establish your beachhead in Canada for your conquering and expansion plans in the form of your settlement in Canada for you and your family.

I know that the last paragraph might have been a little dramatic, but for those who are fans of Sun Tzu and the *Art of War,* you will know that this is the mindset that you need to have to be successful. Obviously, you are not going to attack the immigration department or wage a rebellion as your first act of working to become Canadian, but you must have a plan, and you must be deliberate and measured in having this play out, in order for you to be successful.

At this point, you should have an understanding at the very least about the program sections that are open to you and have a basic understanding of what your best option will be to press ahead with. Once you have this, then you have everything you need to start making some decisions.

In constructing your plan, we want to talk about the components and why these are integral to your success, and the sections that we use for the immigration blueprint are as follows:

GOAL FOR CANADA

I always ask people to be clear on what their goal is for Canada and how they see this process going if it were going as smoothly as possible. I think that this is akin to any type of mission statement with any type of project or undertaking. It is not possible to have a plan without a raisan d'etre or a charter statement for the plan, and this is no different. There are no rules with this statement, and it is surely individualized for the person and the applicant.

I always suggest that people have one main goal for coming to Canada, and then list three to five secondary goals that they have. This allows them to galvanize themselves and their family around the process and be able to use this as a motivator for them to take and follow through on the action.

TIMEFRAMES

In having any type of goal, this needs to be defined with a timeframe (preferably realistic), and since there are so many things that are going on and that need to be taken into account, this should be well defined. Some of the areas with respect to timeframes that need to be taken into account are, the time it will take to be able to assemble the application, the time that the government will need to process the application, and the timing required for the transition to Canada.

You will also need to look at other things that might impact this, for instance, a child aging out on their application as they will no longer be a dependent, or a child that is in a country that has mandatory military service and you would like them to be in Canada prior to this date so that they are not subjected to this, or even something like planning the landing to coincide with the settlement of your child so that their schooling in their home country or their new country might not be impacted.

There could be other instances as well, such as not wanting to shock your system coming from a warm climate to landing in the middle of winter, or for instance, knowing timeframes that might be imposed on you such as having to make your landing in Canada within one year of taking your medical exam.

PRINCIPAL APPLICANT PATHWAY

The main applicant needs to know their pathway and what needs to be done and planned for to be able to execute on this. Several of the items that were discussed in the assessment will be covered here. For instance, their language scores (should they not be completed yet) will need to be addressed so that the principal applicant will know what is required for their program and how best to be able to meet their required goals. This will be totally personalized depending on the principal applicant's situation and will need to be 100 percent clear, as everything with respect to the processing and acceptance of the file will be covered in this stage.

SPOUSE/ DEPENDENTS

Should you have a spouse or kids, then you are going to need to take this into account. This can affect the principal's application in several different ways, such as affecting points needed on an application, or if they even want to come to Canada, or if they have work or school commitments and how this will impact the principal applicant. There are a few things that will need to be addressed here which will need to be dealt with and the situation with respect to the children and the spouse needs to be considered. I would also like to note that should there be a previous relationship where children were involved this can complicate the application quite a bit as noted below.

POTENTIAL PITFALLS / INADMISSIBILITY

We discussed these in the last chapter, and this will address any issues that will need to be raised or could potentially cause a person harm in their application. If not addressed properly and completed right from the beginning, not dealing with these correctly could be catastrophic for an application. It is imperative that these are dealt with properly and professionally. When dealing with these areas, I definitely recommend that you do not try to tackle these yourself and engage the services of a professional. These deal with a complicated cross-jurisdiction legal system (when you are speaking about criminal inadmissibility) and you need to be *very* structured in how you present your case when the subject of inadmissibility is involved.

When dealing with pitfalls, these can encompass any number of things, and include things that might have some sort of adverse effect on an application. It is prudent to identify them and deal with them right from the beginning, so that they can be planned for and dealt with and do not become a "by the ways" and kill your Canadian immigration chances.

Some other examples of things that will need to be taken into account and should be planned for are a divorce with a previous spouse and bringing a child to Canada. There will be documentation that will be required and needed in order for that child or the application to be successful, and if this is the case this could get *very* complicated very quickly, depending on the country. The legal arrangements in regard to the ex-spouse that are not handled properly could still impact your application. Proof of funds or settlement funds are another example, as people could have things tied up or other financial commitments and they would not know when or how those funds need to be available, and at what times, during an application. This is another common example of how things can go wrong unwittingly for a client who does not understand the laws and their obligations to it.

FALLBACK POSITION

This section outlines the second choice, which might not be the best option, but needless to say, this is an option should there be an unforeseen change in the immigration law or the applicant's situation. This is the fallback position that might be needed for the person to be able to execute on their plan and their goals. Also, there might be some *"lines in the sand"* for a situation that need to be accounted for in the plan.

TRANSITION PLANS

This section should not take away from the transition to Canada in the persons' settlement plan, but instead, it will be required to form the basis of that plan and will be important later on in the drafting of transition pre-planning and planning to get to Canada. This section takes into account unique and personal circumstances. For example, being able to leave and wrap up work or school commitments are a common situation that will need to be addressed.

FUTURE SITUATION

This area is something that comes up from time to time. There should be pathways for reuniting a family with a parent or grandparent as this is something that people would like to plan for. Or perhaps considering a family caregiver or nanny that has been with a family for a number of years and is now part of their family, to the point that they would like him/her to immigrate with them.

I am always quick to remind people that we should focus on establishing them in Canada, but I am also able to lay out any other options that might exist and be required for their plans in the future. It is not my place to dictate what is important to people, and their plan is totally their own, and is customizable to what is important to them.

I would also like to dive into a few more technical issues that need to be taken into account when dealing with an application, and why planning is paramount to this whole process and to your success.

I am always very quick to remind people that think of this process as picking a fight, and one that you don't want to lose. As someone who does not pick fights and is non-violent (but in a previous life earned two black belts in his time in Korea) I know that generally, the person who will win the fight will throw the first punch, and will throw it hard while aiming to put their opponent on the ground. This is what you must do in your application and in your planning and something I will touch on more in subsequent chapters, but for now, what this example serves to exemplify is that you need to throw everything at the immigration officer that you can that benefits your case, to ensure that you prove your case. You throw it hard so that the officer is left with no other choice than to accept your application.

You also need to understand that when you throw that first punch it is recorded in a computer system called GCMS which stands for the *Global Case Management System.* This is the government computer system that will track all of your applications and interactions with the government (and some foreign governments – yes there is information-sharing agreements with different countries) from applications, to updates, to phone calls, to any conversations/ interactions with border officers. You should be fully aware that this can also be used to your detriment, should you ensure that you are not deliberate and measured with your communication.

The first time that you file an application, it is recorded in the GCMS system, and you are assigned a UCI *(Unique Client Identifier)* number which forms the basis of your interactions with the department and will be preserved and retrievable for nine years after your last interaction with the department.

As a professional, I have planned client's applications so far in advance that I have put information in an initial application so that I can point to it years later on a planned subsequent application that we already knew and planned on filing. This is the advantage of me knowing the system and planning in advance for my clients.

Another example of a not-so-well-known tool that is out there for an astute professional and most likely not known by a layperson or a newbie practitioner, is what we call the "program manager's report." The immigration department produces yearly reports which are publicly available if you know where to look. These reports are produced by the immigration program manager (the person who is in charge of the immigration section of a visa post) who quantifies how many applications have been submitted in a particular category and what the approval/refusal rates are per the particular immigration program.

This might not seem like a big deal, but if it is used correctly, I am able to plan ways for certain types of applications that have a better chance of being approved, depending on where and how they are submitted. I take this into account in my planning when I look at the venue that the application will be submitted to and what the trends are with that application.

I wanted to point out that there are a number of tools available to be able to plan with and these are two things that I find to be most important of all of the tools and information that is available. Planning can be done at a very deep level and should be taken into account when you are crafting your final blueprint to your immigration success plan.

As a final thought, if you want to win this fight, this battle, or this game, you need to know how it is fought, waged, or played so you need to make sure that you win. This is done through first having an effective plan that takes into account your battle plan, and then executing, which will be the subject of the next three steps of stage 2 of the process which is *Making it Happen.*

I also would like to make one side note, which is that I personally try to stay away from the word "game," as I do not see my client's lives as a game, but in fact, I see this as a life or death battle for their future here in Canada and one that I play to win. This is what my clients expect of me, and this is the value that they get when they engage my services and that of my team's. Everyone at Maple Immigration Services understands this, and I constantly am hammering this home, as this is another instance of what we do and how we are able to change and positively impact people's lives to come and settle peacefully and safely in Canada with their families.

CHAPTER 6:

THE APPLICATION BUILD™

S o here we are, we have a plan and now we are ready to "rock and roll" and Make it Happen. Exciting, isn't it?

Before we dive in, I want to tell you what this chapter is *not*. It's not that I want to start on a negative note, but I just want to make sure that you understand the limitations that are placed upon me and the challenge that I have in being able to ensure that I get you the information you need, while also being mindful of your time and personalized situation.

This chapter is not a guide on how to submit to a particular program. It is, however, a guide on what and how you can plan across several different programs. There will be certain program-specific items that I will elude to, but again, I want you to know that I am trying to be as focused as I can without being too general out of a desire to get you what you need and follow through on my commitment to you – my reader.

The areas that I am going to cover in this chapter are:

- An examination of what a completed application should look like

- How you should think of the government checklist and supporting documentation

- Being careful about misrepresentation and what it can cost you

- Things that should be in your application which you are not told about

- What should be at the top of your mind when proving your application

After we go into a discussion about these items, you will be able to apply them across a number of different types of applications and situations, and this will give you a guide of what you need to think about and how you need to proceed.

WHAT AN APPLICATION SHOULD LOOK LIKE

Your application is a story and it will be your story (like what Chapter 2 of this book was for me), but it is also a different story, depending on the type of application you are submitting. For example, if you are submitting a spousal sponsorship, you are submitting a love story, if you are submitting a skilled worker application then it is a job/work/resume story, and if you are submitting an application as an investor, it is a money story, about how you have accumulated your business experience and your wealth.

So, keeping this in mind, you need to be clear on what kind of story you are telling and the tone of that story, so that you can meet what is being asked of you. I will be speaking more about this later in the chapter when I talk about the *bona fides* of an application.

For the purpose of submitting your application, and on a basic level, your application will consist of a cover letter, the government forms that are required, the supporting documentation that will be required that may not be obvious (again something we will discuss later at length), pictures, medicals, police checks, and fees for the applications.

I know this sounds kind of mundane but guess what? These are the things that are generally requested and will be required across all applications. The other thing that you must know is how this application will be submitted. Will it be submitted as a paper application, which will be mailed in for processing to an embassy or processing center, or will it be submitted electronically through one of the many online government portals? This is another important consideration as to how the application should be prepared and submitted.

Either way, the components of the application will normally be the same, whether submitted online or by mail – it is just the *type of file* that will be submitted that you need to be mindful of.

GOVERNMENT CHECKLISTS AND SUPPORTING DOCUMENTATION

I want you to know something very important. The checklist is not the law, and you as an applicant have a duty to prove your case. This is what you are *not* told, but sadly, will find out later, should you be one of the unfortunate people who is rejected and then trying to figure out what went wrong because you did everything that you thought you were to do when submitting your application.

The duty is on you, the applicant, to present and prove that you meet the requirements of the program that you are applying for, not on the government officer to figure out cryptically if you meet the program requirements to qualify under the category that you are applying under. I can tell you right now that this should be at the forefront of your mind, no matter what application you are submitting, because if you do not do this then you are putting yourself on very thin ice.

So, what does this have to do with the application checklist? *Everything!* There is a saying that I have and that is *"If I only follow the checklist for a client then I am not serving my client,"* as this is only the barebones of what is required and part of the secret to a successful application is not following only the checklist. All of the extra things that need to go into your application to prove your case are not even listed on the application. Why is this important? Well, I believe that this allows for a faster, more streamlined process, as it allows the officer to finalize the file and clear it (yes they are tracked on their clearing rates and want to move files out the door), while at the same time, it minimizes work and the follow-up required for the client and the file.

Always keep in mind that what matters in immigration is what the law on the Immigration Act says, *not* what the checklist says. You need to make sure that you meet what is required so that you can pass the completeness check (we call this the R10 check), and this is the purpose the of the checklist. Then, after you make it past this administrative triage, you must satisfy the officer, and this is a combination of what is found on the checklist, your supporting documentation, and how well you put together an application.

In keeping with this theme and in proving your case, you need to take every opportunity to do this any way that you can, as you are dealing with a faceless system that bases your life on a stack of papers that you submit to a stranger. You must take every chance to impress upon the decision maker why you meet the program and who you are as a person. Any way that you can do this, you must do it.

As an example, when I fill out forms, I don't care if it says only to fill out the form in one way or another. *Nope!* For me, I use any venue, like a fill in box, to explain or advance my client's case. I know that the officer will have to read what I write, and if I can use that to give more information that supports my client's case, or advances their application, no matter how many times I am saying the same thing, I will do it.

With respect to supporting documentation, I have a phrase that was put so eloquently by a colleague of mine many years back when she said: *"Give them more than they ask for so that they can't point to what they don't have."* I loved this so much that, immediately upon hearing it, I sat down at the computer, opened Word, and wrote it in big font, and printed it off on a piece of paper. To this day, that same piece of paper, unframed and crudely stuck to the wall of my processing team's office, is stuck there and shown off to everyone. Thank you, Janice, for those words, as they mean a lot!

Another technique that I use is that I look at myself as if I was in the shoes of the immigration officer, and I ask myself if the information presented answers my questions, or if it creates more questions, and then I work with my client to satisfy my "internal immigration officer."

I also look at it as a skeptic, and I sometimes get worried when things look too good. I have had many times where I look at an application that I am going to submit, and it is so flawless that it really does look too good to be true, and this causes some worry. I take comfort in the fact that it is true and accurate, but I am still concerned that I am not meeting what is required of me.

One caveat that I would like to add is that I also try to seek balance when I prepare an application because I do not want to go crazy with paperwork and make the decision maker angry. I want to make sure that I am keeping their job easy and doing their work for them. If I turn in a file that is hard to follow or creates work for them, what do you think their mindset will be like when they have to give a thumbs up or a thumbs down? Think about that too when preparing and "over submitting," as it really is a balancing act.

Lastly, I would like to give a shout out to a colleague of mine who taught me a lesson that I carry with me to this day. The person that I am referring to is a retired immigration officer (who now works as an immigration consultant), and she taught me that you need to be mindful of the person on the other end of the job who is receiving your application. Working in a government office can be a thankless job with a mountain of applications that never stop. You need to make sure that, depending on the application, you are respectful of their time. In some highly trafficked visa posts, the officer must review and decide in as little as ten minutes on whether they will approve or reject an application. You need present your case, make sure that you are poignant and clear, while also working to do the job of the officer and meet the bona fides of the case (yes, there is that word again) in the program that you are applying under.

As much as this is an adversarial type of process, with me being on one side of a government officer, I do not actually see it that way as I feel a collegial relationship where my government colleagues have a job to do and one that carries a lot of responsibility as do I. We are all there to ensure that we fill our roles but at the end of the day we are good people who want to do what our jobs demand of us.

Therefore, I always have made it a point to thank an officer when I receive good service from them. To me, their job is always filled with complaints, and I will surely be the first one to not only complain when there is an issue, but I will also be the first to say what a good job/ experience something is when it works out that way!

MISREPRESENTATION

This word is akin to the devil in the immigration world, and it is something that you need to be aware of. There are different ways to misrepresent (misrep) an application, and these are defined under Section 40 of the Immigration Act. You need to be aware of what is important to your case (this is probably the only time in this book when I will quote the act directly because it is that important):

(1) A permanent resident or a foreign national is inadmissible for misrepresentation

(a) for directly or indirectly misrepresenting or withholding material facts relating to a relevant matter that induces or could induce an error in the administration of this Act;

(b) for being or having been sponsored by a person who is determined to be inadmissible for misrepresentation;

What this means is that if you declare something on the application and it gives you benefit under the act (i.e.: qualifies you for something when without this misrepresentation you were not qualified) then you have just misrepresented yourself and, if called out on it, then the act goes on to state:

(a) the permanent resident or the foreign national continues to be inadmissible for misrepresentation for a period of five years following...

This basically means that you have been very naughty, and you are now banned for five years for filing another application, and I assure you that any future applications will be looked at *very* closely, as you have now been caught in a lie. Five years is significant (previously it was two years) because this is more of a punishment for you since, by effectively removing you for a period of five years, this most likely will affect your ability to apply and qualify under many different economic programs.

Also, it is important to understand that this misrepresentation can be far reaching. I mentioned previously that data is shared amongst different nations that have agreements. This is the kind of stuff that is shared and can impact you on future applications with Canada, or other places as well, where your information may flow.

Lastly on this topic, there are a few more things about misrepresentation that you must be aware of. If you are thinking of engaging the services of someone who is not licensed (and yes I am begging you not to do it), or if you are being told by some shady consultant or lawyer who is licensed (and yes unfortunately they do exist) that it is OK to leave something off, please run away as fast as you can. The way that this works is that the government will never be able to tag that person with the misrep, but you are the one that signs the form, so you are responsible for the contents. The buck stops with you. But why would you even think that it is a good idea to pay someone who is going to get you into trouble?

If you get a sense that they are fishing for a misrepresentation in received communication, stop! If you are processing your file and there is any inclination that this is an issue and you are being requested to submit more info, you need to stop right away and get professional help. This is akin to you going in for questioning and the detective is just "having a conversation with you" (aka trying to get more information to prove his/her case) about a crime that they are looking at you for. That is the time that you stop talking, ask for representation, and then do things the proper way as opposed to thinking you are being helpful to someone who is trying to gather proof to use against you.

You might think that you are being helpful, but in fact you are giving the officer *"the rope to hang you with"*. You could inadvertently be giving the officer the ability to ensure that he/she has all of the info in order to justify the decision they are working to make against you, when in fact there might be more to the story that needs to be added into the file. I am not saying that you must lie or find someone to dig you out of your lie (if in fact you did this knowingly) but there might be some ways to present the information/reasons why something was submitted in a certain way. Thus, it is in your best interest to get professional help at this point to articulate your submissions as they will become part of your permanent record.

IT WILL FOLLOW YOU FOREVER

A lot of people aren't aware that there is no time limit on a misrepresentation under an immigration application. Should this misrepresentation come up, even when you are a citizen twenty, thirty, or even forty years later, under the current law, you have a potential to lose everything. An aggressive government could take issue and take action against you on this very point. So again, this is very serious, and this is something that you need to be hyper-aware of.

If there was a misrepresentation on a previous application, you need to come clean, but carefully. I have some self-represented clients who have, on previous, temporary types of applications, told a little lie – either unknowingly, or through an unlicensed representative that may or may not have known or cared that they misrepresented an application. I always tell them that they need to absolve their sins and confess (although carefully), as continuing on with the misrep, especially on to a permanent application, will cause more issues. It will also have the effect of ending my representation of their file, as I cannot professional proceed on an application that I know is false. Many will be afraid, but I coach them on the ramifications, and assure them that I will stand with them and they will be fine. I can tell you from experience, I have never had an issue with this, and this has set them free from their past transgressions.

THINGS THAT SHOULD BE IN YOUR APPLICATION THAT YOU ARE NOT TOLD ABOUT

Following with the theme of this chapter, and from the previous information that was presented above, I wanted to point out a few things that you should consider putting in your application, and I really concentrate on two items that are key to your application – the cover letter and the index.

THE COVER LETTER

When I craft a cover letter for an application, all of my letters have the same basic components which serve the purpose of presenting a clear and concise synopsis of my case. It is important to make this as easy as possible for the immigration officer so that they can make a decision about your file. When done properly, this is your summary, and it allows him/her to examine and take the guesswork out of your application. The standard components of my cover letter have the following:

- The applicant's information, which is comprised of their full name, address, birth date, and UCI (if they have made a previous application).

- A statement of what the applicant is asking for and what program type they are applying under, and I want to be clear about what they want and what they are asking for to be granted.

- The qualifying criteria of the program and how they meet that criteria. This is laid out, and in some cases in bullets with sub-bullets, as to how they meet it or for larger programs. I will have these as sections where I will explain in detail how they will meet the requirements.

- Any other considerations that need to be addressed in the application and might cause the officer to question something.

Then, I can lay it out and use it as a chance to explain so that they do not have to draw their own conclusion.

THE INDEX

This is more for convenience of the reader, as it allows them to see what has been submitted and the number of pages that have been put in for the section as well. I also would suggest that you make sure that you number all of your pages, that way, if a page should go missing (and it does happen), then it is easier to show that a particular page was lost. This would need to be taken into account if you are looking for some reconsideration[6] if things go off the rails.

WHAT SHOULD BE AT THE TOP OF YOUR MIND WHEN PROVING YOUR APPLICATION

There are a number of things that you need to take into account when you are doing your application, but first and foremost you should keep in mind what the goal of the program is and what you must prove to meet the requirements, or the bona fides, of the application. You need to make sure that you are always asking yourself if you are meeting the program objectives and if you are showing that you are qualifying with respect to the criteria.

Equally important, I always work to back up everything with as much information as I can, even if it is not on the checklist, so that the proof of what is said is in the documents. This reminds me of a phrase that I always bring up to my team and what I used to tell my students when I was teaching the immigration program for a brief time at a local college here in Canada. I would tell them to *"Never believe your clients, they are liars. But to believe their documents, as the*

---

6 Reconsideration basically means that you are asking for a file to be re-evaluated by another officer or by a Program Manager for instance.

documents never lie. ”

I would say this for a few reasons. Sometimes people would forget a date or be unclear with something on their application, and a document would say something else. I am always mindful of the story that is being told and I want to make sure that the documents that in the applicant's application are telling the same story. If they aren't, then there is an issue, and this leads to a conversation with my client so that we can either supplement or we can explain to an officer why something is the way it is.

Always remember that if you make a statement it should be backed up with evidence. Your word in not good enough. You must always look to supplement with documentation because this allows the officer to give your statement credibility, and this could tip the balance in favor of your application having a favorable outcome.

Remember that it is always safer for an officer to say *no* if they are not convinced than *yes*. If they make a mistake and let someone in who is not supposed to be there, then this can cause problems for them in regard to their fitness in their job. This will also create a high cost because the country will have to deal with the problem at a later date, should there need to be removal proceedings to deal with an officer's mistake. You need to keep this in your mind and make sure that you give them no reason to refuse your application.

SOME FINAL THOUGHTS

As you can see from this chapter, putting the application together is not just about following a checklist and checking things off. There are a number of considerations that you need to take into account and consider when you are putting the application together. Make sure that you stay focused and always remind yourself of the story that you are going to tell. Most importantly, when you are making a statement about something, back it up with evidence. This is always helpful and makes saying *yes* for the decider a whole lot easier.

CHAPTER 7:

THE TACTICAL SUBMISSION™

Are you excited right now? I know I am. You have done all of your planning and we have put together your application! Now we are ready to pull the trigger and execute on our plan with the government processing of your file, and this can either be a lot of fun or not a lot of fun. Kind of like that roller coaster ride that I have described in previous chapters, but I know you have been listening and you are prepared.

In this chapter we are going to discuss the following areas as they pertain to the processing of your application:

- Reviewing your application and preparing to submit

- How to submit your completed application

- How to gauge your application timing

- How to respond to and submit requests for information

- What happens if you're informed of an intent to refuse, or are refused

I think that after covering these topics, you will surely have a better-than-average understanding of what happens in the "black hole" of file processing in the immigration department.

REVIEWING YOUR APPLICATION AND PREPARING TO SUBMIT

The process of reviewing your application prior to submission is imperative. You must do this right up until you send it with the courier (if you are submitting a paper-based application). There are a number of things that you must keep in mind.

UPDATED FORMS

Right before sending in your application, you must check your forms to make sure that they're up to date. Should the forms change (which the department likes to do unannounced) then you must change and update your forms. If you don't submit the right version of your forms, then your file will be returned as incomplete and, in some cases, this can cost you two months, and set you on the track of being out of status if you are in Canada and ending your current status in Canada. It is also advisable to check the form versions (look in the bottom left hand corner for the form version). Then, I like to print off a copy of the webpage that shows the forms and their versions, so if a mistake is made then I can match up the print-out to the courier receipt, and then respond accordingly to the immigration department so that the error can be fixed.

CORRECT FEES

You must make sure that you have paid the correct fees. If you make a mistake, then guess what – that's right – your file will be returned and, in some programs, this will cost you months of time, as you will need to go back into the cue. You do have the option to not pay your RPRF (Right of Permanent Residence Fee) until later if you are concerned about cash flow, but it is advisable to pay this fee at the beginning, as this will keep things moving quickly and, should you be refused, the fee will be refunded to you since that portion of the fee was not used.

KEEP COPIES OF EVERYTHING

You *must* keep copies of your entire application, scanned or a hard copy, whichever you see fit. It is imperative to make sure that you have copies so that you know what was submitted and what you did or did not have in your package. I can describe a bunch of scenarios about why this is important, but I know that you can see clearly the importance of having copies of anything you submit. I would also suggest that you keep copies of your courier receipts. These are also important pieces of evidence and may become increasingly important, should there be a problem and you should you end up finding yourself in federal court. More on that later.

SUBMITTING YOUR APPLICATION

There are two ways to submit a Canadian immigration application, and they depend on the program that you are applying under. The application can either be submitted via an online portal, or it can be submitted via courier to an intake center. Each method has procedures that need to be taken into account.

ONLINE

When submitting online, you must make sure that you have a good scanner and adjust items within the limits pertaining to the standards of the document size imposed upon you. These can range between 2.5Mbs to 4Mbs depending on the portal that you are using and the type of application that you are submitting.

You should also make sure that you follow the directions closely and look at what is needed to submit and how it should be submitted. For example, some applications have very specific rules, such as, if you are submitting a police check online, you must scan it in color. If you scan it in black and white, they will refuse your application. You may be asking, *"Are you serious?"* Yes, I am 100 percent serious and so is the immigration department.

The client information box is your friend. I stack as much documentation in there that I need to. This is a catch- all, and remember, we talked in the previous chapter about over submitting, well this is where you do it when you are filing online applications.

You should also be aware that, due to the limitations of the system and some narrow nomenclature used in the titles, I am never confined by these sections. Everyone's case is unique, so I need to make sure that I submit what is required to prove my client's case. It does not matter if you choose the wrong box, as you need to make sure that you submit the documents required to prove your case.

For your reference we are seeing more and more applications being converted over to an online submission method and the government has indicated that this will be the new norm for all submission of documents. This certainly makes sense, considering the world that we live in.

BY MAIL

There are some rules when submitting a paper application. Firstly, by the time that you submit, you should make sure that you already have the full application copied and the correct forms and payment. This can be harder to get right in a paper-based application.

Next, you need to know the importance of the courier that you will use. There is one major difference when it comes to couriers, and this has to do with the difference between a private courier (such as FedEx or UPS) and a Canada Post courier, which is a Crown corporation, and thus owned by the government. The major difference boils down to the date of receipt, and this is very important when you need to meet a specific deadline. There are court cases (or case law as we refer to it) that have been decided on this very specific question. Generally, the rule is that when you submit with Canada Post, your date of receipt is the date that they take control of your package. It would be advisable to have the postmaster stamp your application (and you will notice that the post office and the mail room at the receiving facility have the same postal stamp – weird, eh?). When you use a private courier, the date of receipt is when the package is received in the mailroom at the processing facility.

So, the reason that this is important is that you need to make sure that if you are under a time crunch and you need to hit a deadline, you need to ensure that you strategically plan how you will send an application.

GAUGING APPLICATION TIMING

This is going to be very hard for you to hear, but it is quite difficult for you to know or be able to gauge your application processing time, even when the processing times are posted online. These online times represent 80 percent of the applications that are processed in that category and tend to not be of much assistance. The other thing that you will do is to jump online and read messages in forums that may be dated or may be totally different, depending on the persons unique situation, and this is a very inaccurate source. Don't do this. It just creates doubt and sleepless nights.

I always let people know that this is the "black hole" and I give them best "guestimates" as to what we are seeing, but again, these are not accurate. Fortunately, I have another tool up my sleeve. I belong to closed professional forums and Listservs, where there are thousands of lawyers and consultants who update constantly about the processing times that they are experiencing with various applications. In my younger years, I studied for my pilot's license out of interest. In learning about weather sources, we were taught that there are many different sources, but one of the most accurate were PIREPS (or pilot reports). These were the most accurate because they were from pilots who had just flown through an area and could give an accurate report. I find the information that I monitor from colleagues to be my immigration PIREPS. They show me how fast a certain visa post or program might be moving, and they give me data on certain trends that may be happening at a certain time. Application processing tends to slow down in the summer months and over holidays. I am going to guess that my government counterparts enjoy their vacation time as well, and this leads to a slowdown in processing and your application.

So, the short answer is, I would not think too much about application processing and resign yourself to the fact that the application will be processed as it should be processed. You will put yourself through a lot of sleepless nights otherwise. Hang in there. You are not alone, and the immigration department knows it. We are told from the department that they are looking at and experimenting with ways to solve this issue, but don't hold your breath on it. We will believe it when we see it and when we see it works.

HOW TO RESPOND TO AND SUBMIT REQUESTS FOR INFORMATION

Normally, when a request comes, it will come in the form of a letter, in an email, or through your online portal, and it will have directions as to how to respond. When given multiple options, it is always advisable to respond in specific ways, so that you ensure that the message has been received (since the onus is on you to respond).

I would strongly suggest that you make sure that you document your submission in the following ways:

- If you have sent this via email, you will have a copy, but we will always BCC ourselves on the request and then print and add this to the file.

- If you are submitting via the government webform, you must make sure that you take screenshots at every page and every submission, as these are date-stamped, and they will be required.

- If you need to submit by mail, make sure that you have a cover letter with your application details. Put in a copy of the request letter along with the requested documents and make sure that you keep complete copies. Ensure that you send this via courier within the requested time, and make sure that you keep the receipt (take note of the information about the different types of courier options and what to take into account).

- If you are submitting via the application portal, then you should upload the requested document to the slot that has been created and be sure to keep screenshots of the upload.

WHAT HAPPENS IF YOU'RE INFORMED OF AN INTENT TO REFUSE OR ARE REFUSED

The short answer is to retain professional services right away, and I mean *right away.* There are specific rules that need to be followed, and, believe it or not, there are errors that happen. They can be corrected if you know how to do it. It would not be prudent for me to explain them here. This could be a whole other book topic and not one for an untrained professional.

What you need to know is that, depending on when, where, and under what program the application was submitted, you might have the chance to raise a rejection to the program manager or case review in Ottawa. At the same time, you will need to also weigh out the type of error that was made (if there is, in fact, one) and what you have to lose as a result. This will then dictate your next course of action, which would be an appeal (if that is open to you with respect to the application that you submitted) to the IRB (Immigration and Refugee Board). Or, you may need to preserve your right to file an application for leave with federal court to challenge the government in a proceeding, called a "judicial review."

Again, as I am sure you can gather from this section, determining the correct option is very complicated and should involve the strategy devised from a trained professional. They will give you all of your options, and it would be advisable to work with a professional who specializes in the needed area.

FINAL THOUGHTS

At this point, the only advice that I can give you is that your application is now out of your hands and in the hands of the decision maker. If the job has been done correctly, then you should be in for a smooth ride. If, however, there are some issues that come up, you will need to know how to react. Either way, there is nothing that you can do, and this is now out of your control until you hear back. So, trust in yourself (and your representative if you are using one). And, if you have a religion, then trust in whatever god or energy force that you believe in that things will unfold as they should.

CHAPTER 8 :

THE LANDING EXPERIENCE™

Congratulations! You have joined a select group of people who have successfully filed and been approved for their immigration application. This has cleared a path for you to come to Canada as a permanent resident. You are almost finished with a major milestone, but there is still some work to be done, and you cannot take this newfound status for granted. You are not a permanent resident until you land in Canada and your status is confirmed on your landing document. Until that time, you are not approved, and things could still go backwards.

I am not telling you this to scare you, as the chances are small, but I have seen this happen a few times over the years for different reasons.

The topics that we will cover in this Chapter are:

- You have been approved – *yeah!*

- Documentation you will receive for your permanent residence.

- What happens between my approval and my landing in Canada?

- What will happen when I land in Canada at the airport?

- What are my obligations as a permanent resident of Canada?

YOU HAVE BEEN APPROVED!

Once you receive your approval letter, this is the time that you will need to finalize your application processing. On this letter, there will be instructions of how to finalize your application. In general, you will be given a process to follow that includes where you will send in your passport or a copy of your passport (depending on your circumstance). Additionally, you will submit pictures of yourself and your family. All of this will be submitted through a VAC (a visa application center) or you will be given instructions as to where the requirements will be mailed in. If you are sending in a photocopy, you will need to have an ETA (electronic travel authorization) prior to coming to Canada. This is necessary in lieu of the sticker on your passport and can be done online.

When this is being done, the government office will give you a landing document, which is the exact document that you will need to become a permanent resident of Canada. This is one of the documents you must have when you arrive in Canada and will be needed in order for you to land in Canada and start living your dream life as a permanent resident.

DOCUMENTATION YOU WILL RECEIVE FOR YOUR PERMANENT RESIDENCE

There are two main documents that you will expect as a result of finalizing your landing in Canada. These include your landing document or COPR (Confirmation Of Permanent Residence) and your PR (Permanent Residence) card.

YOUR LANDING DOCUMENT

You and each member of your family will receive this document, and what you will notice is that it will have all of your vital information on it. You need to make sure that all of the information is correct, as this will need to be changed prior to your landing in Canada. You will also need to make sure that you take into full account the validity of the document.

It is *very* important that you land prior to the expiry of this document because there will be no extensions. If you miss this date and arrive after the date on the document, you risk going back to the beginning of the process of applying and starting all over again. You will also notice that this document will need to be signed. Don't sign it when you receive it because you will need to sign it when you are landing at the port of entry with the BSO (which stands for the Border Services Officer). At this point, you will then become a permanent resident of Canada, and all of the rights of this will be granted to you at this time.

I cannot stress enough that this document is *extremely* important, in fact, irreplaceable. So please treat this like a treasured possession. I always describe this to clients as your non-replaceable birth certificate, as this is really what it is. This is your first document (like a birth certificate) where you have been born again into your new home in Canada. This document sets the stage for all of your identification and the beginning of all of the benefits and rights that are attached to your newfound status.

THE PR (PERMANENT RESIDENT) CARD

This card is nothing more than travel document, and I cannot say that enough. Most people think that it is their PR and that when the card expires so does their status. I field a number of frantic calls where people will say, "Oh my god, my PR is expiring!" When, in fact, it is only the card that is expiring. The purpose of this card is to allow you to board a commercial airliner. You do not lose PR status when the card expires. The only way you can lose your status is if it is taken away from you, or you decide to give it up and go through a formal process where you give up your permanent residence by renouncing it.

So, what is important to know about this card, is that it allows you to travel and must be used if you are travelling on a commercial carrier. You will not receive this card at the airport when you land, but this will come about six to eight weeks later and will be mailed to your address in Canada.

This is important to know as if you are landing in Canada and planning to leave shortly thereafter. You should plan to apply for a travel document at the Canadian Embassy (a whole other process) in lieu of your PR card. You should also make sure that you have a secure address for this to be delivered to while you are not away, as this will need to be supplied at the airport. You must also know that it is *highly* unadvisable to send your card through the mail outside of the country.

I know that people do it and in the old days had no problems, but be aware that there are means of detection in the card that can be screened in the mail system, and you risk having your card confiscated and sent back to the immigration department with you having some explaining to do. I am not telling you this to scare you or to be over-cautious, but I am telling you this based on experience, as I have seen some clients get themselves into this very uncomfortable mess.

WHAT HAPPENS BETWEEN MY APPROVAL AND MY LANDING?

We have already gone over some of the basic procedures leading up to your landing and covered the key documentation that you should expect, but I would like to draw your attention to some other things that will happen prior to your landing. A lot of this will be covered in the next chapter and should comprise a good part of your pre-settlement plan, as you will have a number of very individualized tasks that will be required at different stages of the process. For this stage, prior to leading up to your landing, there will be lots of emotions that you will have to deal with. You may feel excitement about the new adventure and the thought of your goal/dream coming true. Or doubt might enter into it, as you are diving into an unknown and you might question if you are doing the right things, or you may even have second thoughts about your success.

These are all normal. You should not worry about these questionable thoughts, as you can take solace in the fact that you have planned and that you have always had success up to this point in your life. That is why you are here where you are now.

You must make sure that you put in the work on your pre-settlement plan and that you have a clear goal and articulated plan prior to your landing. If you don't do this, you will pay for it later, and it could be a big price.

You must be mindful of your packing requirements and what you are bringing to Canada. You need to have all of the key documentation that you need to have with you, but you should also be filling in your customs forms, as you are allowed to bring a number of items in, duty free, or have them follow later, tax-free, if they are coming with you. It is advisable that you prepare this documentation and make sure that it is ready and well thought out, so you are not taxed on personal items in the future.

In the meantime, leading up to your transition, enjoy your last moments in your current place of residence. Take in all of the things that you wish to do (maybe that one tourist thing that you said you would always do but never did because you lived there). Have all of those last dinners with your friends, family, and well-wishers, as you are about to make this journey *very* real!

WHAT WILL HAPPEN WHEN I LAND IN CANADA AT THE AIRPORT?

You have gotten everything together and you are hopping on the plane to land in Canada. You are *very* excited and possibly nervous at this point, as you sit in your airline seat with your significant other, your family, or just you and your thoughts. It will become very real once you are handed your customs form (yes, some flights still have these). With that, the "fasten seat belt" sign starts to blink, and you hear the announcement to return your seat back up and stow your tray. Yep, that's right, in a few minutes you will be touching down in your new home.

The plane doors will open up and you will deplane as you may have done so many times before, but this time, it will be different, as you will not breeze through customs or that very non-talkative border officer. You will be beginning your first day as a permanent resident.

When you are filing through the airport, you will come to the arrival's hall, which, depending on the time of day, will be in either a state of chaos or a state of sleep. You will then either go to a machine, or you will meet with an officer at a booth, which is called the PIL (Primary Inspection Line) booth for all of you high fact finders that love this type of information. You will tell him/her that you are here as a permanent resident, and they will then direct you into a place called "secondary." Secondary is a room (and, depending on the time of day/ year, might be in a similar state of chaos or sleep) where you will hit the pinnacle of your journey to this point. This is where the border officer will have more time to deal with special cases that require that extra bit of clearing, such as landing a permanent resident.

You should also know that this area is used to issue work or study permits (watch out in August as it will be busy), and also deal with people who may be claiming refugee status or who might have been a little bit naughty and who are being investigated for things like smuggling, etc. Don't be alarmed if the place is busy or if chaos ensues (as it certainly could), but pay it no mind, because this is *your day!* Don't worry if you witness any number of different emotions, from happiness to sadness, as you can see it all in this room, depending on what the officers are dealing with that day. I just wanted you to be aware of where you are and what could happen. Remember my job is to be your guide in order to take the mystery out of this process at every stage.

For you, this will be a place of happiness, as this is where you will meet with an officer and they will confirm your permanent residence – a rebirth, if you will. Your first day as a resident of Canada. Wow I think I got caught up in it there for a minute. But truly, this is a special day, and one that I have been lucky to see first-hand from my clients who have made that journey and have changed their lives forever. For now, let me guide you through the rest of what will happen in secondary.

After you have let the person know why you are there, you will wait in a line until you are called up to what is generally a big counter. The officer will then confirm your details on your landing record and then he/she will ask you to sign the documents and then they will stamp them. It is at this point that you are now a permanent resident of Canada. *Cue the confetti and music! Yeah for you!!*

Depending on the time of day and where you are landing, you might be able to check getting your social insurance card (SIN) or tax number off your settlement plan list. Some ports have a Service Canada location setup for you, so that you are able to save yourself the trip to another government office and move things forward.

You will then go down and collect your baggage and possibly be subjected to a customs inspection, where they will look for any items that you should not be bringing, and make sure that you don't have any of these items. If you do, you'll be in the computer and will be inspected every time you come back to Canada if you get caught with them without declaring them. This will be a *big* pain in the butt for the next seven or eight years for you and for anyone who is travelling with you.

At this point, you have completed your landing and you will be quite tired, so it is time to rest and get settled until you move on to your landing and settlement list (which is covered in Chapter 10 of this book).

Note: For this section, I have chosen to highlight the procedure of what will happen when you land at an airport, as this is where most people will have their permanent residence confirmed. However I would be remiss if I did not mention the two other options for landing, and they are relatively the same except for each venue, such as if you are arriving at a land border and driving into Canada, or if you are doing your landing inland. I will cover the differences for these as they are minor, and the landing mechanics are roughly the same.

LAND BORDER

Everything will be the same as landing at the airport except you will be driving in a car. You will drive up to the booth where the primary inspection line will be and then you will tell the officer that you are wishing to land as a PR. You will then park your car and proceed inside to meet the border officer, who will conduct the same procedure of landing you. I would like to point out that specific ports have rules about how many people they will land in a given day, or which days they will conduct the landings, and they are not published generally. It is *very* frustrating and ridiculous that this is allowed to happen. There is no way that I can advise you on how to mitigate this, but I did want to flag it as that is all I can do at this point for you. Hopefully the government agency in charge will find a way to balance this in the future.

INLAND

This process will happen if you are finalizing your permanent residence inland, as you are already here. This will be coordinated with an office in Ottawa who will send you a landing appointment and direct you to a government office at many different locations throughout Canada. At this point, you will be given a number and then will meet with an immigration officer at a wicket, who will go over your document and then finalize your landing. This might not the same type of experience as landing from a plane as it is very *"administratively dry."* Nonetheless, the result is the same result.

WHAT ARE MY OBLIGATIONS AS A PERMANENT RESIDENT OF CANADA?

Congratulations! You are now a permanent resident and you have made it. You are now out of the airport and are settled into your transitional housing, and you are so happy that you have made it here to this point.

You may have had the border officer tell you in his/her speech that you have obligations as a permanent resident, but I would like to go over the main ones to make sure that you are clear on what those are. I want to be clear that as a permanent resident you are *not* permanent in the sense of the word, as the most important word is "resident" – many people don't understand this until they are confronted with it. Actually, one of my previous client's terms it as you are a "permanent guest." If you get out of line, the government can still ask you to leave, like any bad guest. The only person that this cannot happen to is someone who is a Canadian citizen.

RESIDENCY REQUIREMENT

You must make sure that you meet this requirement as this is the one and only thing that you must do. You need to make sure that in a five-year period you are here for two years. What is also important to understand is that the block of time that is the five-year period for the residency requirement is a moving block of time. Most people don't understand this very important detail.

What time effectively means is that, as time moves forward, so does your accumulated stays at the beginning of your time, so they will effectively erase. They will stay the same or erase if you are not in the country. In short, those five years are a moving five years, and you must make sure that you have met two years within a five-year period or are able to meet two years within the time that you have left in that period.

So, if you come, land, and then go home after a month, make sure that you are back here, at the very least, three years later. The biggest ways that your residency can be reviewed is by a very diligent border officer or if you apply for permanent resident renewal or foolishly think that you are qualified for citizenship.

I would suggest that you keep track of all of your trips and time in and out of Canada with a spreadsheet or even just a notebook. I would also suggest that you retain all of your boarding passes (not tickets – easy to fake), so that should these come in to question, you have that evidence that we have discussed before when you were putting your application together.

NOT GETTING IN TROUBLE

So, we all know that you are a good person. I would like to hope that you are not going to get yourself into trouble. But mistakes do happen, and if you enter into any legal issues you *must* consult an immigration legal professional. Sadly, I have seen people create problems for themselves by taking the advice of their criminal lawyer (who was doing their best in their area of law), but as he or she is generally not fluent in immigration law, what they thought was best for their client sent them on a course for putting their time in Canada in jeopardy. A great example of this is getting a DUI and then pleading it out, which makes you inadmissible under the Immigration Act and then the border services agency can start proceedings to strip you of your permanent residence.

Sure, you might think, "Come on, how can they do that?" Well, I kid you not, I have seen this, and other things happen over the years that I would not have believed if told to me. Another crazy example that comes to mind was an eighty-year-old Italian lady who came to Canada as a small child in the 1950s. As you get older and retire in Canada, it is common to spend winters in the warmer areas of the United states. Well, she was doing exactly this, but she never became a citizen, even though, after many years here, she felt like one and was behaving as such. As she was spending more and more time in the United States, she was away for longer periods, and, as it turned out, she missed her residency obligations.

After eighty years in Canada, and travelling back and forth, she thought nothing of it, but guess what the border officer did? He started proceeding to strip her of her permanent residency. Can you imagine how she must have felt going through this at the border? I can tell you, by the time I was called, she ended up having her travel plans thwarted for a while and spending lots of money defending her right to stay in Canada.

SETTING YOURSELF UP FOR CITIZENSHIP

Citizenship is the goal for many, and one that is required for you to have "tenure" here in Canada. What I mean by this is that you have been given rights that are very hard to lose and are not the status of "*permanent guest*" anymore. I always tell people (including my previous example of the Italian grandmother), that if you are planning to stay and make a life here in Canada, your citizenship is a *must* for so many reasons that people don't think about until they are confronted with them. This step is not as onerous as it might be in other countries, but this will surely give you "*tenure*" and give you the much-coveted rights that are sought after the world over. This is certainly something that you should plan for if Canada is the place that you intend on calling your home. But again, this is another conversation that needs to be looked at strategically due to your home country's requirements and your long-term plans.

FILING TAXES

All I want to say to you is that you need to file taxes as a permanent resident, even if you return to your home country after arriving. Make sure that you take this into account and find a competent professional to help you. I could not impress upon you more the importance of working with *a true* professional in all of your affairs, and an accountant is surely one of those whose job is to make sure that you are able to maximize your tax benefits while minimizing your obligations. If you have a good person, they will pay for themselves and then some.

At a very basic level, you are able to do everything a Canadian citizen can do while you are here in Canada, except join the military or vote, as these are reserved for citizens. I am very proud of you that you have made it to this point in your immigration journey. You now only have to decide if you will take that final step as a newcomer to Canada and get that Canadian passport. At this point, you do not have to worry about this, other than following what has been outlined here and you will be fine.

CHAPTER 9 :

THE PRE-
SETTLEMENT
FORMULA™

Pre-settlement planning is something that you may not have thought of when coming to Canada. Most will only start to look at this once they have *"checked the box"* of getting approved for their visa. This is key to your very ability to settle in and make a smooth transition to Canada. I was lucky that I had experiences of helping people and guiding them to settle, prior to them actually arriving in Canada. I learned from what I saw about people who were able to make that transition as well as with others who struggled. Guess what? It really boiled down to who was going to put in the work and who was not. This is what this stage and what life is all about.

Lastly, I want to point out for you how important pre-settlement planning actually is and how the government only just started to take notice of this a few years back when they launched a pilot program for people to complete prior to landing in Canada. I was so happy when they *finally* did this in conjunction with some settlement agencies, but it surely took a while for them to get this sorted.

Our process in pre-settlement planning is education, and the plan that we put together has major areas that need to be addressed. It really picks up where your immigration blueprint leaves off. I have decided to lay out the plan and their sections with descriptions of the items that need to be considered[7].

SETTLEMENT PLAN MISSION

As we spoke about in your immigration blueprint, you must have a clear mission visible with any plan and it must be personalized and well-articulated to meet the settlement goals and the goal for you and your family in all areas of your life in Canada. The mission forms the basis of the plan and to your entire settlement transition.

SETTLEMENT GOALS AND TIMEFRAMES

What does a successful transition look like to you? There is no wrong answer, but this shows what the goal will look like and allows you to measure your success. This is really turning your success into something quantifiable, so that you can look at your plan and what you are measuring yourself against and can clearly execute the goals of what you are trying to achieve. A big section of this is timing. Your plan will be adjustable and dependent on the time that it will take you to get settled in. This will be closely tied to a number of different factors and will take into account such things as your work or family commitments (special days, school, work obligations), timing of the PR, the medicals, and how you will transition everything over (i.e.: will you come to meet your PR obligations and then go back and bring things in at a later date).

EDUCATING YOURSELF ON CANADA

This is fundamental and is quite easy to do when you are getting ready to come to Canada, as there is the great tool called the internet. This might sound boring, but you really need to understand your new home. A simple history lesson will allow you to understand certain things about the country that are translatable today. By taking the time now to get this understanding (something that children get

---

7   Go to www.mysecondpassport.ca/settle for some settlement information & useful resources

in school here), you will better understand how to settle into the country. It will also make you a little bit more relatable when you are doing things like looking for jobs, because you will have a deeper understanding of where you live.

Again, this should be fun and can be enjoyed by the family. You are lucky that you can get lots of this stuff from YouTube, if that is how you would like to consume your content (like most people). Or you can simply watch the news or read the newspaper to understand the issues, which is something that you should really consider, even prior to coming to Canada.

LOCATIONS

Canada is quite diverse. You need to understand if the region that you live in is closely aligned with your values, your career, or your language and culture. You need to understand that these issues are quite real and that they can be clearly defined by geography. A great example of this is that someone in Vancouver is more in line with the thinking of someone from California, as opposed to someone from Toronto or Montreal who may be more in line with the thinking of someone who is from New York, per se. Even though we're separated by a border, these differences are pervasive and can be explained by geography. When thinking about location in Canada, you need to be strategic in your planning for your family and your career. Just hopping on a plane from Toronto to Vancouver can be the better part of a five-hour journey, depending on the weather and which way you are going. Plus, you are crossing three time zones, so you need to be clear about where you are living and what goal this serves for you and your family.

PREPARING YOUR FAMILY

This section really takes your family account and, above everything else, you need to make sure that they are on board and involved in the process leading up to this big move, especially with respect to getting settled in. As noted in the previous section, educating them and getting excited is a good thing because there will certainly be some attachment challenges that everyone will wrestle with, especially when you are launching yourself into the *"unknown."* This can be exciting and should be framed as such, but you need to make sure that you have a clear plan for them and how they will be able to settle in to school, their community, and their life in general. This section is all about them and their needs.

PREPARING FOR YOUR CAREER

There is a lot you can do to prepare prior to leaving. This is where you can have the most impact. I can tell you that very few people hit the ground running in this area, unless they have already laid the groundwork and put in the time to invest in their career. I can also tell you that this is where most of the issues and stresses come into play.

The good news is that you can have the most impact prior to arriving in Canada in this area. There are a number of things that you can do to prepare, depending on the job that you do. For instance, if you are in a regulated profession, then you can start to prepare what is required for internally educated professionals in that profession. All of this stuff is available on the internet.

You should look to what professional groups would have the most impact on your job prospects and start to network and connect with other professionals in a deeper way. Remember that you already have a network in your home country that you can leverage, but now you need to build that network again and make sure that you are able to maximize your time. There are a number of ways to do this, but you should ensure that you take the time to do this.

You might want to consider is a career change, if this is what you want to do. With coming to Canada, this is new for everyone, but you need to make sure that you have a realistic plan which might include you starting that business that you have always wanted to start, or maybe even going back to school in that career that you wish you had. Whatever is best and achievable for you is all fair game.

BUDGETING

This is *very* important. You are going to need to know what money you are working with and then you are going to need to make sure that you can meet your obligations. In this plan, you will be looking at what the spending will cost you for your transition, and how you can make money while you are in this transition period. This could include a staged transition where one person settles and the other will continue to work in their home country until they can move (a popular plan that may or may not be wise). Or you might want to find a transitional job that will supplement while you are moving into your career. Again, not a bad idea, but you want to make sure that you are not hurting your job prospects either.

Having a financial plan in place is key. This, along with your job transition, will be your biggest source of stress if you do not properly plan and execute. A note of caution on this as I always see a few of the same mistakes. The first being that they are not investing in themselves or their career and they are trying to hold on too much to their funds out of fear. This has held them back from advancing faster in Canada. Another mistake that I see is that they will become a *"human currency calculator"* where they will be still in the economic system of their homeland, which might be a lot cheaper than what they are spending.

It was always somewhat humorous to me, watching some of my Indian clients who had just arrived from Delhi, doing the math in their heads about the cost of a tea at Tim Horton's, and how shocked they were at the cost. I would always politely remind them that the minimum wage was more than the daily rate of a labour job, and that they should stop thinking in this manner because they would be caught between two very different worlds.

ONE-MONTH AND ONE-WEEK CHECKLIST

Prior to arriving, we suggest that you put together your one-month and one-week checklist and make sure that you have certain items on your calendar for taking action. This can be planned well in advance, but you know that when one month until your arrival comes, that you will be executing on the tasks and already have the tasks defined and time set aside to cover them. It is important that you know what needs to happen at different milestones. Pressing the "go" button in these areas will require you to act on certain tasks that will be dependent on other tasks. This will be tied into the timing of your plan and what will be required for you to do at different stages to meet your time commitment.

Additionally, depending on how you are going to transition, you might not want to start applying for jobs, if you are too far out from your landing, but you might want to start to meet some people in order to ensure that you are starting to get your name out there for the future. Again, this section as with your whole plan, should be highly customized depending on your situation, your plan and is certainly different for everyone.

ON THE GROUND TO-DO LIST

This will be broken down into deliverables that you will execute once you land. This list will allow you to go through and systematically get done what you need to do. This will include things such as hooking up government IDs and the like, to more personalized tasks, but either way you will know what you are doing. Rest assured, this will be covered in greater detail in the next chapter, so you will have a clear understanding of this section.

LONG TERM PLANNING AND GOAL SETTING

This is something that we always ask people to do as if there is a long-term plan for the future this could impact what they are looking to do from the beginning. I personally find it useful to define my long-term goal or aspiration and then figure out how I will get there and what needs to be done. This is what this section is all about.

As an example, if your intention would be to work in the oil and gas field in fifteen years, it might not be prudent to move into Montreal at this stage, unless there is a good reason (and a family member is not always a good reason), as this will cause great expense and uprooting of your family. Being clear on your future goals is necessary for your smooth transition down the road.

FINAL THOUGHTS

Going through this process is a very individual and personalized process and you need to be the one to put it together. We always ask our clients to do this work so that they can then check it and get feedback from a professional depending on their plan.

This should be fun, as this allows you to lay out the life that you want, and you can have whatever you plan for. You have a ton of resources out there to support you, but you need to know where to find them and how to best use them to your advantage for your individualized plan. There is no right or wrong here. All that matters is that you think about what works best for you and your goals and what is realistic for you to be able to achieve at the given time. I would also suggest that you involve your family in the planning, as they are coming along with you and you should be fully aware that they are as equally invested in the plan. This can be a good family bonding exercise for you and with older children because this allows them to get excited about their move and be a part of this life changing process.

CHAPTER 10:

THE SETTLEMENT ADVANTAGE™

You have landed in Canada and have ticked off a very big check mark on your to do list for life and in achieving your permanent residency. Congratulations again but you are now on to the part where the *"wheels can fall off"* yet again if you are not careful and strategic with your first moves in your new homeland. I know that I sound like a broken record, but this is for good reason, as I want to make sure that you understand how important this is and not be lulled into a sense that you are there yet because you are not.

The good news is that prior to you landing in Canada, you have already taken my advice by putting together your structured plan that will form the basis of what you are about to execute on. In this chapter, I am going to give you an overview of several different topics as they relate to executing on your settlement plan. Some items are more important and pressing if you are planning on staying in Canada, while other tasks will come more into play later when you return to Canada.

GOVERNMENT SERVICES AND HEALTH CARE

This will be your first step. Much of what you will need to process ahead will be your government IDs. There are two "must get" IDs that you must have and then two more that are advisable. Normally, when you are applying for these, you should have a trusted address. If you are working with transitional housing (something I will cover below), make sure that you put this on your list to change over your ID addresses when you move, as some government organizations will only communicate via mail.

SIN (SOCIAL INSURANCE NUMBER)

You get this from Service Canada, which is the service arm for the federal government. Some countries call this a tax number; a TIN number; or tax ID, but for us, we call this the SIN card. This will allow you to pay your taxes (yeah!) but it will also allow you to work and get some of the government benefits that are available to you, such as checks in the mail to support the upbringing of your children.

HEALTH CARD

I would only like to talk in general terms about this as healthcare is administered provincially. and, as such, there are numerous sets of rules with respect to when you can apply. In Ontario, for instance, you need to have been living in Ontario for ninety days before you can apply for your health card, whereas if you are living in Alberta for instance, you will qualify upon landing. Again, it is advisable that you get this right away to ensure that you have adequate healthcare options in place. If you have to wait, then you should be setting up private insurance prior to leaving for you and your family.

DRIVER'S LICENCE AND PHOTO ID CARD

A driver's licence may be an easy or difficult thing for you to get depending, on which area of the world you are coming from. In some cases, you can just do a straight swap for your licence and start driving, while in other places, there will be a process and some testing that will be involved. Again, this is a provincial program and something that will be part of your pre-settlement planning. Should you not get a driver's licence, that is fine, there is another piece of ID that is not as known, and this is the photo ID card. This purpose of this card is to give people photo ID (clever name, right?) when they do not have the ability to get a driver's license. These IDs are important because it can replace your passport as your main form of ID, as your passport should be in a safe place.

BANK ACCOUNTS AND CREDIT ESTABLISHMENT

Getting a bank account is *very* important and a key part to settling in. This should be something that you do in your first week. I would suggest that you check around, as you will find some very good packages for newcomers because the banks are very aggressive to woe you for your business. You should be able to get free services (some banks up to a year) with some giving you a free safe deposit box and others that will also help facilitate your first Canadian credit card.

I also want to tell you that some banks will give you a credit card for $500 and then ask you to put a $500 deposit down as security. This is absolutely insulting and something that you should not consider at all. Why would you pay interest on your own money? Again, you might want to hold off on the credit card until you have employment, as it will make it easier to have no security, but I wanted to let you know that this is not something that I would ever advise.

Lastly, I wanted to highlight your credit and the importance of keeping it clean. In this country, you can get money quite easily if you have good credit. I know I have people chasing me to give me credit cards and loans, as they are trying to make money from me. Make sure that you keep this in mind. Having bad credit in Canada will affect you in so many areas of your life, from being able to purchase high ticket items to being able to rent a place to live. Credit checks are standard when you want to rent a property. Lastly, you will find that in Canada, not having a credit card makes life somewhat challenging as you are unable to access many of the great services that are out there, but again just be sure to treat your credit like "gold" because it is.

FINDING PROFESSIONALS TO ADVISE YOU

One of your priorities is to surround yourself with professionals. I know for me this is my number one priority in life, which is to find good people who are good at their jobs and can provide valuable service to me. I would like to highlight the importance of a few for you so that you can keep these in mind.

I like referrals myself as this always works best for my peace of mind, but I also look at who I am going to be most comfortable with, and who I feel that I am comfortable putting my trust in. This is similar to many of my clients when they are on their immigration journey and they decide to put their trust in me.

REAL ESTATE

Finding the right agent who will be invested in helping you find a place to live, both temporary and permanently, is key. You want someone who is obviously not after the commission, but someone who will be invested in what is best and most affordable for your living situation. From a personal standpoint, I have my guy who knows the area well and has a good network of professionals that I will need for any deal, and he has years of proven experience. You should be looking for this in your real estate person. Also, you should know that this person will generally work for you for free as a buyer or renter. They are paid on a rental (one month rent as commission is the norm) paid by the owner, and they earn their commission from the seller if they are selling you a home. So really, they are providing free services to you, so just be respectful of their time.

ACCOUNTANT

I would strongly suggest that you find a *great* accountant, and not someone who is new to the industry either. Getting a personal tax return completed for an annual filing should cost you between fifty and one hundred dollars with a competent person, and when they get cheaper, it can get a little scary. This person, if they are professional and up to date, will save your money and let you know how best to navigate the system. I would warn you to be careful with the larger places that specialize in tax returns. These companies will hire a large bunch of contract workers, put them through a training course and then release them to do your taxes with little other experience. I appreciate that people have to start somewhere but it should not be with your tax return. You can find a seasoned professional who will be there year after year and understand your situation for roughly the same price.

BANK REPRESENTATIVE

This person is very important because they can make things go a lot smoother when you are applying for a financial product through a bank. They can tip the scale in terms of a yes for a financial product, so by getting to know them and them getting to know you, you have nothing but value to gain.

INSURANCE AGENT

You might want to consider this, but I would suggest that you are quite careful with who you are choosing to represent you. I am sure you already know these people are a dime a dozen and you need to be very mindful to make sure that you are working with a professional. There are lots of people who have very little clue about what they are actually doing, and they are only in this profession to make as much money and sell as much as they can. I know you are smart about this, but I wanted to say it either way.

FAMILY DOCTOR

Another necessary professional to have is a good family doctor. You should be aware that these sometimes can take quite a long time to get as there is a "shortage" of doctors, and thus you will find it is common to initially be told that they are not accepting patients. You should not be discouraged. Generally, you can get a referral from a friend to their doctor and they will be able to accept you. Or you can sign up on their list and be persistent, and they will then take you on as a patient. I know that this may sound strange, but this is what happens, and you need to be aware of it.

HOUSING, SCHOOLING, AND TRANSIT

Where you are going to live is dependent on so many things. In general terms, you should know the area that you wish to live in and the city (this should have been sorted out in your pre-settlement plan), however, at this stage on your journey, you need to be open and nimble as to your living situation until you know the areas that you are working in or where your children are going to school. It would be advisable to rent a place initially (maybe even Airbnb for the first month) and then transition into your full-time community once you are more settled. This is wise, especially if you are living in a larger city, you'll want to be aware of commute times with respect to your living conditions. Also, if you have children, this is even more complicated because you'll want to be mindful of the connections that they will make in school. You don't want them starting to feel settled only to be uprooted again for another school and another area.

REGISTERING YOUR CHILDREN IN SCHOOL AND IMMUNIZATIONS

This would be a priority for you if you were arriving and staying during the school year. There are some clients that I have had who look to live in areas where they have found schools that they felt would be higher quality (tip: there are ratings of public schools that you can look at to find schools that are quite good). With that said, public schools are generally quite good, and they have to adhere to a standard curriculum that is given to them by the province. You might want to keep in mind that you should have immunizations up to date and check in advance/bring any documentation as this will be required for school admission.

DECIDING IF YOU REQUIRE CANADIAN EDUCATION

Canadian education might not be a bad idea and something that you may wish to consider, depending on your settlement plan and what you are looking for. There are some very unique educational and professional certification options that you can take which will lead into a job quite quickly or that second career that you may have already taken.

Some other benefits to education is that they can be short in duration, have flexible schedules to accommodate your work/life schedule, they can come with co-op options which allow you to work with an employer (and be paid in most cases) and then transition into a job. I know as an employer I like this, as it is a long interview for the person, and I can see how well they will fit into my team or not. You will also find that there are some very excellent student loan options that will allow you to study and will fund you at the same time. You can also develop a network of other people through school that might be an asset to you in the future

GETTING AROUND IN CANADA (DRIVING VS TRANSIT)

You need to decide if you will need a car. If so, then you are going to need to take into account the cost, what insurance will look like for you (generally this will not be cheap), and the benefits that having a car will provide for you in terms working and living. It is quite difficult to advise you on this area because really this boils down to your personal situation and your location. Where I live, not having a car would make life quite difficult and almost impossible. But if you are in an urban area, with a good transit situation, then having a car is not really necessary at all, but it depends on your commute.

You should also be aware that there are a number of car-share services out there, where you can use a car for a day (to do shopping for instance) or for a weekend, to get away. But you are going to need to have a driver's licence, so again, you might want to take this into account when you are trying to figure out whether to invest in a car or not.

WARNINGS AND THINGS TO LOOK OUT FOR

SCAMS IN YOUR OWN COMMUNITY

I always like to tell people to be careful. People within your own community might target you and you will find that you have *"a new best friend."* They will know about a *"deal"* on the house that might have been a place where a murder took place that they keep flipping to a new person in the community for a loss, for instance. The sad fact is that there are some people who will prey on you because they know that you are new, don't know what is going on, and that you will most likely have money with you. What they don't know is that you know me, and I have already wised you up to this. Again, you're smart and have been around the block a few times, so just smile and know how to keep your distance.

WELL KNOWN SCAMS THAT TARGET IMMIGRANTS

There are scams out there that target newcomers and they usually come in the form of a threatening and urgent phone call, where you will be told that you need to pay this or that and if you don't you will be arrested. What is alarming is that they will have your info and they will also call from a number that is masked and looks like it is calling from a government number. Do not fall prey to this, as this is a well-known scam. You know, from going through the immigration process, that the government will generally only communicate by letter and *not* in a threatening tone over the phone as they ask you to pay at a Western Union or with Bitcoin. I know that we are in an advanced society, but the government is quite pragmatic in their way of doing business, so I assure you that these will not be genuine. Have a good laugh at the person and tell them to come and arrest you!

SORRY, WE ARE LOOKING FOR CANADIAN EXPERIENCE

This always bothers me when I hear about it and you may or may not be confronted with it. I have seen this happen to people that I worked with in the past and I always get very angry because there is even a ruling in the province of Ontario that this is a human right violation, as it is a form of discrimination. This is very hard to deal with and would be very frustrating. You need to be mindful that it is one thing for someone to do it and another for you to have to prove it or go through a tribunal and get a ruling. Again, not something that would be a good use of your time. My best advice is to remember it and use it as fuel to make you stronger. The person that tells you this is obviously not fluent in the power that diversity can bring to their organization.

WATCH OUT FOR YOUR FAMILY AND FRIENDS

I know this might sound strange, but if you think about it, it makes sense. I always warn people to watch out for their family and friends. They generally want to help you, but the problem is that they may not be skilled in the type of help that you need. Just because they did something themselves or they may know something, that does not make them the *"expert"* or the right person for the job, even if they are there to help.

They might have some contacts for you, or they might push you to be close and live near them. That is great if it works for you and your plan, but you need to be mindful that you should be taking a very objective and deliberate approach to your settlement. If you family can help with your plan, then great, but if *your* plan becomes *their* plan then you might get caught in that trap where their good intentions lead you to a bad place.

CONNECT WITH YOUR COMMUNITY, BUT NOT TOO MUCH

I know that there is a tendency to gravitate to what you know and people from a similar background, and this is great when you need a taste of home. But remember the reason that you came to Canada and that sense of adventure you had, getting up and moving, across the world in some cases, to be here. Do not limit yourself to only within your community, as this is a crucial mistake, especially because there are options for you to grow and leverage yourself in different communities and different circles.

DEALING WITH A NEW ENVIRONMENT AND ADAPTING (ESPECIALLY IF YOU HAVE CHILDREN)

This is something that you need to watch for yourself and for your children. There may be some pretty dark nights out there ahead for you and for your family, but you cannot let these late-night demons creep into your mind. There will be a lot of pressure on you to succeed, as your friends and family will be watching from your homeland and will be eager to keep tabs on how well this decision is working out for you. They may be supportive, but they may also be doubting. Nothing is easy in life and you know this, but you have already shown the *grit* to get to this point, so take solace in this fact and keep this in mind. Also, make sure you that you watch your children as they might be putting on a brave face. This transition might be hard for them as well. Lastly, if you feel that you need some help, by all means reach out and get it. This move can be a lot for anyone. Just hang in there and keep resigned to the fact that you are doing this for a better life. If it was easy, then everyone would be doing it.

NOT MAKING AN EFFORT TO UNDERSTAND CANADA OR THE CUSTOMS

This is a huge mistake. You have made the decision to come here. No one is asking you to assimilate or forget who you are or where you came from, but you must make an effort to understand the customs because it will allow you to relate to many of the people that are here. Even though people come from different places on the planet, we are united as Canadians, and not just through our love of maple syrup, coffee, and poutine.

This chapter was put together based on some of the more popular things that I have witnessed with clients who have had to settle in. I will say it again, settlement is one of the most crucial steps of the process and one that I have paid particular attention to when it comes to my clients and their journeys.

CHAPTER 11:

THE CITIZENSHIP SOLUTION™

So here we are at the final stage of *The Immigration Success System™*. It has taken years for you to get this to point, and this is the final stage of your immigration journey where you will get "tenure" and solidify your place in Canada for good. I always refer to this as the "tenured" position.

I use the word "tenured" very deliberately as I think that it is an appropriate illustration of the situation, and if you would indulge me in drawing this parallel for you, I think you will agree. When you are on Temporary status (a student or a worker), you are basically a Teaching Assistant as you are really temporary and can go anytime. When you are a Permanent Resident, you are basically a sessional instructor as you have a little bit more stability but you may find that should there be a shift then you may lose your spot; but when you are a tenured professor, you are truly permanent and it takes a lot for you to lose this status, just as it does to lose your job at an academic institution. Citizenship is your tenure in the immigration process.

I find that most people mistakenly think that once they are physically in Canada, they have arrived, and while this is true to a certain extent, their Canadian dream could very easily go wrong if they are not careful, which is why I am very quick to correct people when I see them thinking this way.

Most people don't know that even as a Permanent resident, they can still lose this status quite quickly and have proceedings started against them that will, in turn, see them returning to their home country and risk them losing everything that they have built over their sometimes years in Canada. I know that you might think I am trying to scare you and most do not even pay this a second thought as generally, these are exceptional circumstances, but I would like to give you a few scenarios that I have seen over the years:

The first one involves a woman who was in her eighties at the time. She came to Canada from Italy at the very young age of four years old with her parents, who decided to find a better life in Canada. As was the case in the 1950s and 1960s, there was an influx of Italian immigrants to Canada who were seeking better opportunities for themselves and their families. Fast forward 75 years, this lady was well settled in Canada, but she had become what we affectionally referred to in Canada as a "Snowbird," which are older retires who chase the warmer weather in the US by heading to warmer climates. Well, as it happens, she was spending more time in her home in the southern US than in Canada and, in fact, she was not meeting her residency requirements. As she has been here for so long, she took her status for granted until that fateful day that she crossed the border and a very astute BSO (Border Services Officer) started a report against her to remove her Permanent Residence status. While unlikely that she would be removed and sent back to Italy, the proceedings were started and this not only upset her life and her travel plans, but it also came at great expense of stress with a financial cost to legal representation.

The second scenario involves a guy who was married to a Canadian woman. It was around holiday time and they were pulled over for a roadside Breathalyzer at a roadside stop. He, unfortunately, had one too many holiday libations and blew over the legal limit, and even just the small amount he was over led to being charged with impaired driving. He then went through the system and retained the services of a lawyer. The lawyer in advising him properly in the criminal context did not consider his immigration situation (as most do not take this into account) and the case was settled. The person thought that everything was completed and finished—wrong! It was only when CBSA (Canadian Border Services) initiated proceedings to deport him to his native country that he realized the failing on the part of his criminal attorney — in the immigration context, driving while impaired is considered a serious crime and makes him inadmissible to Canada. I can't even begin to tell you how much cost and stress this created for this family.

Now I do appreciate that you are a law-abiding citizen and probably not thinking about what life will be like seventy years from now, but I illustrate these two scenarios to emphasize the importance of being as educated on everything related to immigration and citizenship as possible.

CITIZENSHIP BACKGROUND

The Citizenship Act is a body of laws that legislates Canadian Citizenship and in fact, this is a different set of legislation that has regulated your immigration journey up to this point. Previously your immigration journey was defined under IRPA (The Immigration and Refugee Protection Act). The Citizenship Act has not been revised and remained quite consistent over the years except in 2017 when there were some major revisions.

Throughout this book, I have not gone into depth about the requirements for different immigration programs, as this was never meant to be a program-specific book. Immigration is a highly fluid field and is always evolving and changing. With that said, I am going to take a brief departure from what I have previously done and give you some of the brief requirements that you will need to apply as a citizen.

I am only doing this as the requirements have truly remained quite consistent with little variation over the years, and I would expect that they will remain consistent for future reiterations of the requirements. Also, it is important to note that the prerequisites that I am going to lay out for you are the general stream, as this is most likely the path you will be following when applying for your citizenship. You should be aware that there are different pathways to citizenship for people who are born overseas to Canadian citizens or requirements, depending on a person's age.

THE BASIC REQUIREMENTS

If you are one of those people who are wanting to secure your passport right away and want to do it quickly, the soonest that you can start this process after being physically present in Canada is by being in the country for 1095 days within the 5 year period prior to your application date. Basically, you need to be in Canada for 3 years and be filing taxes.

There are some exceptions to this rule, and this was a major change in the most recent revision where they brought back a rule that allowed you to gain an extra year of residency as a temporary resident (a student or worker). How this works is that during the time prior to permanent residency for each day you are here in Canada, you will be credited a half-day towards your citizenship for upwards of a year. So, if you were here for two years prior to becoming a Permanent resident, then you will be able to apply for your citizenship one year sooner as you would have one year credited towards your time. How awesome is that?

I would also like to draw your attention to some exceptions to the residency requirements that might allow you to be able to become a citizen. I have one client that I was able to get citizenship for after submitting an application with far less than the required days. In his situation, due to his work requirements, he would not be able to ever meet the requirements and thus, there are mechanisms in place to account for this. Oh, and if you a professional athlete that needs citizenship to be able to compete in the Olympics for instance, you might find that your citizenship gets a little extra attention.

Lastly, I know that you are an upstanding member of society, so I am quite sure that you will not break any laws as if you do or if you spend any time in jail in Canada or abroad, then this will affect your ability to become a citizen.

THE LANGUAGE TEST

You will need to show that you have nominal proficiency in one of the official languages (either English or French) to be able to become a citizen. This is an area that a lot of people fear, and I think that this fear is a little misguided. I find that whenever this comes up over the years, more than a few people enjoy this part of the process as much as giving blood or having teeth extracted and will look for different ways to get around this. There are not many ways to get around this except with some of my older clients who wait to age out. Yes, that is right, you only need to take the Language test if you are between the ages of 18-54 at the time you sign the application, so if you are older, you can certainly wait it out if you so wish. Again, without getting into specifics (as they may change), the scores required are quite low, so with a minimal amount of work, you should be able to navigate the process.

THE CITIZENSHIP TEST

Yes, that is right, you are going to have to do a test as they want you to at least have some basic information about the country that you have decided to make your permanent home. The topics on the test cover history, geography, the government, the laws, symbols, and the economy. The test usually takes about 30 minutes or so to complete and are either multiple choice or True and False. There are many ways to prepare for this test, with materials being found online from the Immigration department as well as others who have put together Apps that you can use to test yourself. I have obviously reviewed this to be familiar with what my clients have to face and also enjoyed studying with my wife who had to go through and successfully complete her test as well. The information is quite basic and again not something that you should fear as all you need to pass and meet this requirement is 15 out of 20 questions right.

THE PROCESS

So now that we know what the requirements are, I would like to give you a really high-level overview of what the process for citizenship currently looks like.

Once you have assembled all of your requirements, you will prepare everything, and have it submitted to the government office that will process this particular type of citizenship application. Currently, this is a paper-based application, but as the government is changing over to more of an online application submission-based system and given the nature of the program requirements, I would predict that this might actually turn into an online application process in the very near future.

Currently, the process starts as of the date your application is received. Following receipt, you will be mailed notification that the application was received, and then you will have two major items that will be requested. The first one will be providing fingerprints, and the second is going to take the citizenship test discussed above at a citizenship office close to you. After you meet these requirements, you will then be invited to the final step in the process and in your immigration journey, which will be your citizenship ceremony, something I will address later in this chapter.

A final processing note that I want you to be aware of. Previously, this process was straightforward where the officer would work with you if your submission was somewhat deficient. As an example, they would ask for documents to be updated if something was not right. Since the change in the Citizenship Act in 2017, this is anything but the case as now you must meet the requirements for a completeness check, which is a similar provision in the Immigration Regulations. The reason why this is important is that we have seen a lot of people's applications returned. It is at this point that a lot of clients will engage my (or another professional's) services—one person that comes to mind had her application returned three times before she finally figured that she was in over her head and needed professional help. Again, this is certainly very frustrating for the layperson to go through and can have ramifications as well.

SOME OTHER CONSIDERATIONS

There are a few reasons why you might not get your citizenship on the first attempt, and while most will carry on with the process of getting their citizenship, there are some that will choose not to for various reasons. The reason that I generally see people make this decision is that their home country does not allow them to have dual citizenship or carry two passports. Another reason that I see is for tax or business reasons. Again, these are very personalized due to the individual and may change over time.

A warning for your grandchildren and any children born outside Canada who you think might have a claim to citizenship. I want you to know that there is a law in place that only affects people when they find out about it, usually as a refusal from the department.

Often people think that their child is a citizen but only finds out that they do not qualify as they, the parent, was not born in Canada. An example of this (that I have seen a few times recently), is if you come to Canada and you become a citizen with your family, and then your son or daughter falls in love overseas after taking on a job. They then decide as most do with their children to return to Canada, but they find out that their child is not actually Canadian as they themselves were not born in the country, and the child was born overseas. This nuance to the law has created a lot of heartbreak and led to serious problems for a number of people who are unaware that this law exists, and I only bring this up to keep in the back of your mind should you find yourself in this spot in the future.

A FINAL WORD

The benefits of the Canadian passport have been touched on at various times throughout our time together, but I want to give you some of the tangibles again. You are now truly a member of this great country, where you can vote, run for politics (or even Prime Minister) if that is what you want, join the military to represent Canadian interests abroad, and most importantly know that you now have the right to enter Canada and never be denied access to your home.

More than that, as a Canadian citizen, you have access to all of the overseas counselor services, the ability to obtain government assistance with your business through trade representatives, and take part and use all of the trade agreements that are open to Canadians.

I was born in Canada, and while I have never had reason to go through the citizenship ceremony myself, I am lucky as I have been part of this process with my clients and also with my wife. I can tell you that this will be one of the most memorable days of your life and an important one for the history of your family. You have worked very hard to get to this point in your journey, and this will truly be the end of your personal journey. However, it may not be the end of your time with the Immigration department as you will find that you might want to sponsor a relative or help someone to come here after learning first-hand how great Canada will be for you, your family, and for your future generations.

Congratulations! You have been on a long journey, but you have now successfully completed a major life goal by getting your Second Passport. You are now proudly Canadian and tenured.

CHAPTER 12:

WHY PEOPLE STRUGGLE

As we draw closer to the end of our time together, and as I have worked hard to lay out what I do as a professional while articulating how I am able to help people succeed with their dream to settle in Canada, I would be remiss if I did not also address some of the biggest challenges that I see with people. This is in regard to people actually following through and being able to execute on this very complicated legal process.

This legal process has many details that can impact you negatively at every turn, and what is even worse about this, is that a lot of these are hidden in various documents that no untrained professional would even know about. There are procedures that are not even published, and I only know about them because I can access internal government documentation to understand what those policies and procedures are. Again, the answers are there but most have no idea where to find them.

I also can not impress upon you more that making one mistake can be fatal in your application, and you need to know how to put your application together and what you need to share, justify, and what is relevant and not relevant without misrepresenting your application.

As you now know, misrepresentation can too be fatal for you and your life in Canada.

NOT KNOWING WHO TO TRUST OR WHAT TO TRUST

One of the biggest issues that I also see is lack of direction as people look online and have so much information and reports from people that have no training, except that they were lucky enough to make it through the system. People get lost in all the noise and waste so much time when they could just be getting it done, as opposed putting their application in jeopardy.

It is hard to know what to trust or who is telling you straight. When I think about this, I think about my tailor in Korea, Mr Kang, who was well-known and very gifted. I would always ask him about this style or that style and he said to me one day, *"Brandon, what I do is make people look good. What you need to do is concentrate on your job so that you can pay me to make you look good."* From that point forward, I never looked back, as Mr. Kang's no-nonsense answer made sense. From there on out he earned my trust and I was happy for it, as he knew how to dress me very well. The point is as that it is hard to let go and put that trust into someone. But there is a point where you have to make that decision and know what you can do well and what you can let a professional do well.

I certainly do not want to end off on a negative note, as that is not who I am, but as you should know now, I have a very direct and no-nonsense approach. I pride myself on serving my clients by being direct and to the point, as this is important in my line of work. One of the hardest parts of my job is seeing people who want nothing more than to make Canada their new home for themselves, their family, and all of the potential that this place has to offer. But because they made one very fatal mistake, they cost themselves and their family that chance forever. This is truly heartbreaking for me and something that I will never get over.

Unfortunately, I only get to meet these people when they have made a mess and then decide that they are in over their heads. Sometimes I am able to help them, but more often than not, they have done so much damage that it is impossible for them to come back from it. It is so hard to see, and there is good reason that I have a Kleenex box within reach in my office, as I will sometimes need to reach for it when the person is in my office and they find out the truth of their situation.

I will never forget one lady that stood out to me as I was writing this chapter. She came to me right around Christmas time with a problem that could have been handled if she had only sought professional help. I told her that we would call the immigration department together and I took the extra time to try and fix this with her right then and there. I knew that the news was not good, but I had to give her the answers that she needed, so together we called.

It was exactly as I expected, that if she hadn't made one crucial error, she would have been fine, but it was way beyond fixing and everyone knew it. Even the person on the other end at the Immigration Call Centre was getting emotional from hearing this lady in my office realize that her simple error cost her, her ultimate chance of staying in Canada as a permanent resident.

This lady was so shocked that she had no other option than to return to her home, that she started shaking so bad that I walked with her down the stairs (as my office was on the second floor) and I was worried that she was going to fall down the stairs.

It is these situations that always remind me the cost of getting even the smallest detail wrong and not being able to come back from it. It makes me so sad to think about the price that people pay. If they had taken the time to get the professional help that they needed, their chance at a life in Canada wouldn't have slipped through their fingers.

CHAPTER 13:

SO, THERE YOU HAVE IT!

We have gone on quite a journey together, and my sincerest hope is that I was able to deliver to you on the promise that I made at the beginning of our time together, which was to give you the information you need to be able to move and live safely in Canada with your family, in your new home and your new life. As you know, I have laid out the process that I have used for over a decade with numerous clients that has resulted in their successful transition to Canada. I have worked hard to give you the advice that is most important to your success, so that you can now start your own Canadian immigration journey and do it properly, in a systematic and informed manner. You can now make educated next steps on what you need to do to take action and take the first step in your own journey. All of this is not theory, but the information that I am lucky enough to use to make a positive impact in people's lives, which is what I am here to do.

I truly hope that now you can now feel a sense of relief that you have gotten the right professional information that can replace those long hours of searching on the internet and wondering how to take action. You now have a holistic overview of the immigration and settlement process that will allow you to be the next Canadian success story.

To look back over what we learned, I would like to do a quick summary of the highlights:

CHAPTER 1: WHY CANADA IS THE PLACE TO BE

We talked about what so many people want and dream about when they set out on their Canadian journey, while at the same time we got on the same page with respect to why Canada is one of the premier destinations for people to immigrate to.

CHAPTER 2: WHY WE DO WHAT WE DO

I was able to share with you the guiding principles and a little bit about my past which has allowed me to grow and understand my clients and their needs. We discussed the ways in which I've been able to impact thousands of lives positively through Maple Immigration Services.

CHAPTER 3: A HOLISTIC APPROACH TO CANADIAN IMMIGRATION

I was able to share my system that I have created which takes an all-encompassing view of the immigration and settlement process and addresses all areas of the process in a systematic and proven approach that we use every day to help people make Canada their home.

CHAPTER 4: THE DISCOVERY SESSION™

We discussed the importance of doing a thorough assessment to make sure that we had all of the information required to determine the easiest, quickest, and most cost-effective pathway.

CHAPTER 5: THE IMMIGRATION BLUEPRINT™

You were given the elements of the plan that we use to set you up for success for the immigration processing stage, which lays out the plan of attack for filing a successful immigration application with the Canadian government.

CHAPTER 6: THE APPLICATION BUILD™

We covered what to collect and what you should consider when putting together an application, while pointing out how things are not always listed for what goes into an application and how you should think about your application.

CHAPTER 7: THE TACTICAL SUBMISSION™

You now have an understanding of how to review your file and some expected steps that you will encounter when processing with the government. At the same time, you learned how to react and protect yourself when your file is in play at the processing stage.

CHAPTER 8: THE LANDING EXPERIENCE™

You have been approved and now it is all about making it to Canada and the steps required to prepare for your landing and get off to a good start.

CHAPTER 9: THE PRE-SETTLEMENT FORMULA™

This chapter outlined the plan that you should create when you are still in your home country so you can hit the ground running when you arrive in Canada and set the stage for your successful settlement into your Canadian life.

CHAPTER 10: THE SETTLEMENT ADVANTAGE™

You understand how to execute your settlement while knowing what you need to do on the ground in Canada and how best to start your new life.

CHAPTER 11: THE CITIZENSHIP SOLUTION™

You have a clear understanding of the final step of the immigration journey which is your citizenship to Canada. We have examined the requirements and some considerations.

CHAPTER 12: WHY PEOPLE STRUGGLE TO EXECUTE ON THEIR CANADIAN PLAN

We had to address some obstacles to the implementation and possible complications that you will face going at this without professional representation.

MY WISH FOR YOU

I would like to leave you with some final words, which is my wish for you. I truly hope that you will remain inspired and become one of the chosen few who will take action right now and make your dream of settling in Canada a reality.

You can make that happen, but only if you move forward, and as we have discussed earlier in the book, if you are qualified and you want to be in Canada, then *do not* hesitate to take the opportunity, as you don't want to lose it.

I truly appreciate you taking the time to read my book. To express my gratitude for reaching out, I'd love to offer you a free class on immigrating to Canada, so you'll have a safe home to build a dream future for your family by starting your new life in Canada. To get instant access go to www.mysecondpassport.ca/secretclass

Thank you for investing your precious time with me, and I hope you will connect with me. Even more, I hope to see you here in Canada, living your dream life soon!

ABOUT THE AUTHOR

Fresh out of university, Brandon Miller left for South Korea, which he thought was going to be a year of teaching English before returning to law school. Instead, he got more than he planned for us this year forever changed his life and started him on the path to having a positive impact on not only his clients and their families but generations to come that will call Canada their home.

It was only by mistake, a little investigation and series of serendipitous events that allowed Brandon to shift gears from the education industry to his Canadian immigration calling. What is most ironic is even as a native-born Canadian with a long lineage in Canada he had to reintegrate himself back to Canada after being away for so long.

He identifies with the same challenges that his clients face, as he returned to Canada with a wife that he now had to sponsor in the immigration system and an infant child that he wanted to grow up under a Canadian value system.

Brandon operates a boutique immigration practice in Toronto, Canada, where he has helped countless people find their way to Canadian shores and settle in successfully to their new home. Brandon first and foremost is a proud Canadian who sees himself as a nation builder responsible for shaping the Canada of tomorrow with its true asset—the people who call Canada their home.